She Shoots...
She Scores!

She Shoots...
She Scores!

A COMPLETE GUIDE TO
GIRLS' AND WOMEN'S HOCKEY

BARBARA STEWART

Doubleday Canada Limited

Canadian Cataloguing in Publication Data

Stewart, Barbara, 1960–

    She shoots ... she scores!

ISBN 0-385-25809-7

1. Hockey for women.   I. Title.

GV847.S74 1998a   796.962'082   C98-931680-7

Cover design by Joseph Gisani, Andrew Smith Graphics
Cover photos courtesy the CAHA and Canapress Photo Service (Kathy Willens)
Line illustrations by John Etheridge
Text design by Heidy Lawrance Associates
Printed and bound in Canada

Published in Canada by
Doubleday Canada Limited
105 Bond Street
Toronto, Ontario
M5B 1Y3

TRANS   10   9   8   7   6   5   4   3   2   1

For my grandfather Duffy, a great

hockey player, and for my grandfather

George, a great hockey fan.

And for all the women ever involved

with hockey, past and present,

for without them this book

wouldn't exist.

CONTENTS

CHAPTER 3

ACKNOWLEDGMENTS

I was an armchair hockey fan until my early thirties when a discussion with my literary agent and friend, Daphne Hart of the Helen Heller Literary Agency in Toronto, changed all that. We were talking about hockey and women … and I saw a light go on! That's how ideas are formed, and that's how this book — and my hockey career — got started.

I'd like to thank Fran Rider of the OWHA and Lynn Olson and Karen Lundgren of USA Hockey for their support and encouragement, and most of all for their love of the game. I'm also grateful to Glynis Peters and the CHA for providing me with valuable resource material and contacts, and to Angela James for teaching me how to skate, and more importantly, how to stop!

Many thanks to all the women who gave me their time and photos for the profiles; you know who you are. Thanks also to Bev Mallory, Melanie McFarlane, Jayne McIntyre, and Mary Ormsby for all their assistance. For the revised edition, I'd like to thank Andria Hunter, Michael Wassman, Karen Kost, Stephanie Boyd, Kelly Dyer, Sue Scherer, Nancy Scholz, Audrey Bakewell, Marg McAdam, Sarah Couch, Karen Kay, Shannon Miller, and Joanne Gray, Susan Demmings, and Danielle Dufour at the CHA. I'm also grateful to Laura Halldorson at the University of Minnesota for her help in procuring the list of women's college hockey teams, and to Julie Andeberhan at Cornell. And not forgetting the men, I wish to thank Jim Geary at Canstar, Rob Spiers at Sports Traders, Darryl Sittler, Ian Young, David McMaster, Rick Polutnik, Russ McCurdy, John Marcetti, and Phil Pritchard at the Hockey Hall of Fame. I'd also like to thank Stew MacFarlane from Abalene, and Kris Pleimann at USA Hockey, for their help in procuring new photos for the book.

I'd also like to thank the professionals at Doubleday, my editor on the original manuscript, Susan Folkins, whose foresight and determination made this book a reality in 1993, and my editors on the revised edition, Pamela Murray and Christine Innes, whose dedication made this new version possible.

Thanks to my mother Corinne for all her inspiring words of wisdom. Thanks to my husband Chris Gudgeon; without his love, patience, and encouragement, this book wouldn't have been possible. Thanks to Tony Nelson — I am so proud that you are my son. And finally, to the three reasons that I get up every day — Tavish, Charlie, and Keating — you make me want to make this a better world.

FOREWORDS

Hockey is a great game, and a Canadian tradition. Women have always played hockey, but more often than not it has been a case of quietly playing shinny in backyard rinks and struggling in women's leagues that received little support, and even less credibility.

Things have changed dramatically, and the 1980s may have been the most important decade in the history of the sport. Determined players from several countries showcased their talent and love of the game to the world in 1987 during the first Women's World Hockey Tournament. And women's hockey became an official Olympic sport at the 1998 Winter Olympics. With this new-found acceptance, young girls around the world have more opportunities to play hockey for fun and friendship.

Women's hockey is unique and deserves strong support and recognition. Some women may choose to participate in men's programs, but this alone does not make them better players; it is the desire to play hockey that matters most.

Congratulations to Barbara Stewart and Doubleday Canada for producing this book. Although women's hockey has been around for over a hundred years, very little has been written on the subject.

Best of luck to all hockey enthusiasts. And remember, the friendships and life skills you gain through hockey endure longer than the victory or defeat of any single game. Good sports are the true champions.

Fran Rider, Ontario Women's Hockey Association

When the young women from around the world stepped on the ice at the 1998 Winter Olympics in Nagano, Japan, the single most important event in the history of women's hockey took place. The participation of these women in the 1998 Winter Olympics was the culmination of over a hundred years of female players striving for recognition and respect from the typically male-dominated hockey and sports world. These Olympians will be for ever recognized as ushering in a new age in female hockey.

All female ice hockey players should not let this historic moment be forgotten; this should be the stepping stone to the next generation of female ice hockey players. The battle for equality and respect should not only continue but grow as our program grows. In the future no female, regardless of ability, age, or desire to play ice hockey on either male or female teams, should be discouraged. The work of those that came before us in this sport should not be forgotten, and the continued work of those presently involved in women's hockey should be encouraged.

This book reflects the continued desire of the author and publisher to educate and inform the female ice hockey world. The information contained in it is vital to the development of new girls'/women's teams and their programs. Only through dedication, education, and information will girls'/women's ice hockey continue its current rate of growth and development. The author and publisher are to be commended and applauded for their efforts.

Karen R. Lundgren, USA Hockey

INTRODUCTION

When I was younger, I used to love Sunday nights. After dinner, I'd rush through the dishes, and then run over to my grandparents' house. My grandfather would be sitting in his favorite chair waiting, for me to curl up on his lap. Together we'd tune in *Hockey Night in Canada* on his tube radio.

I would listen in wonder to the voice of the announcer as he spoke of magical, mysterious men who flew down the ice and caused thousands of fans to jump to their feet and roar and cheer. Who were these hockey players? How did they fly? Any why was everyone so excited?

I wanted to be one of those special people. Well, I could skate, couldn't I? But this was something so different. In those days, a little girl on her grandfather's lap could only dream.

That was over thirty years ago, and my fascination for hockey hasn't dwindled. But now I know there was nothing truly magical about those hockey players; they just did what they loved to do: skate fast, shoot hard, and play hockey.

A few years ago, I joined a women's recreational hockey team, and it's been terrific. Hockey is a great way to have fun, exercise, and meet new people. But best of all, you get to fly down the rink, shoot the puck, score the goal, or, if you're a goalie, make the fantastic save. Play hockey? Why not! There is nothing holding you back. The world will be watching when you score the gold medal-winning goal for your Olympic or professional league team.

CHAPTER 1

Women's Hockey: Yesterday and Today

The Dawsons versus the Victorias, April 13, 1904. Note the long skirts and woolen sweaters.

Hockey Hall of Fame Archives

HOCKEY HISTORY IN A NUTSHELL

Organized hockey has existed for over a hundred years, although the roots of the game go back many centuries. Originally, hockey was played on frozen lakes and ponds just for fun. Games with rules didn't evolve until the 1880s.

The earliest known image on film of women involved in a game of hockey features Isobel Preston, daughter of Lord Stanley Preston (of Stanley Cup fame), playing hockey on a flooded lawn in the winter of 1890.

No one is sure when the first "real" hockey game was played. There is evidence that in 1853 some of Queen Victoria's soldiers, bored by the long winter, played a game of field hockey on a frozen pond at Windsor Castle. The Queen herself apparently watched with great delight.

Despite this royal romp, most hockey historians believe that the game developed in Canada during the late 1800s. A group of students from Montreal's McGill University first put the rules of hockey on paper. Borrowing from lacrosse, field hockey, and rugby, they came up with a rough-and-tumble version of hockey, with up to fifteen players on each team.

The first hockey games used a ball instead of a puck. But the ball bounced too much on the ice. One day, someone had a bright idea: they trimmed the top and bottom off the ball. This left them with a disk that slid smoothly across the ice. Over time, this disk came to be called a "puck," a word supposedly derived from the Old English word meaning "to poke or hit."

The origin of the word "hockey" is also something of a mystery. No one knows who first coined the term. We do know, however, that the name comes from a variation of the word "hoquet," meaning "hook." This makes sense, since the long sticks used in both field and ice "hookey" have hooks at the striking ends.

Queen of the Ice, circa the 1920s.

Hockey Hall of Fame Archives

As the popularity of hockey spread, people began to take the game more seriously. Various leagues sprouted up across North America. In 1892, the best teams in these leagues challenged each other for the first Stanley Cup. The champions were a team called the Montreal AAA.

For the next twenty years, any team could challenge the reigning champions for the Stanley Cup. In 1913, the process became more formalized. The top team in eastern North America played the top team in the west. It wasn't until 1927 that the Stanley Cup became the sole possession of the National Hockey League (NHL), which had started ten years earlier.

In the forties and fifties, professional hockey was more popular than basketball and football — only baseball attracted more fans. In Canada, hockey grew to almost mythic proportions, thanks to the magic of radio. Foster Hewitt's weekly *Hockey Night in Canada* broadcasts were heard by millions of hockey fans from coast to coast and helped to cement the image of hockey as Canada's "national sport."

Since the sixties, hockey has just kept going and growing. In 1967, the NHL doubled in size — from the original six to twelve teams. As the seventies unfolded, hockey became so popular that a rival professional league, the World Hockey Association (WHA), flourished, competing with the NHL for both fan support *and* some of the biggest names in the game. Bobby Hull, Gordie Howe, and Wayne Gretzky all played for the WHA. In 1980, the two leagues merged under the NHL banner, creating a new league with twenty-one teams. The NHL continued to expand in the nineties, and in 1998 had 30 teams.

Today there are thousands of hockey teams across North America, Europe, Japan, and even in such unlikely places as Saudi Arabia. Everyone, from three-year-old kids to ninety-three-year-old grandparents, is playing and enjoying this sport.

Hockey Hall of Fame Archives

Bank of Montreal team of 1920–21.

WOMEN IN HOCKEY

Women have played hockey since the game began on the frozen lakes and ponds more than a century ago. Just as men's hockey became organized in the late 1880s and the early part of the twentieth century, so did women's hockey. A photograph in Canada's National Archives shows a girls' team from Barrie, Ontario. The date on the picture: 1892. In 1894, a group of young women at

The Preston Rivulettes, LOHA Champions,
1931–32.

Hockey Hall of Fame Archives

McGill University decided to hit the rink for weekly hockey games. The school gave these students its blessing, along with the following three conditions:

1. They had to have a guard at the dressing room door.
2. No men could watch.
3. They had to be "comfortably and warmly dressed" in long skirts and heavy woolen sweaters.

With these restrictions, it's no wonder the women soon looked for another place to play. However, these young women had started something big. Over the next four years, women began playing organized hockey in places such as Kingston, Ottawa, Regina, Victoria, Montreal, and Quebec City.

Numerous leagues flourished in Canada and in the United States during the twenties and thirties; there was even an East–West Championship tournament reminiscent of the old Stanley Cup challenge series. One team from this era stands out: the Preston Rivulettes. They were Canadian Champions from 1930 to 1940, playing over 350 games and losing only two, an amazing achievement for any sports team.

For quite a few years following World War Two, people seemed to lose interest in women's hockey. The post-war years included setbacks for the progress women had made in sports, hockey in particular. It became very difficult for a young player to find a competitive girls' team. In 1956, a nine-year-old named Abby Hoffman made headlines across Canada. The reason: the boys' hockey league she was playing in discovered she was a girl and they banned her from playing. But the story has a happy ending — as a teenager, Abby turned her attention to track and field. She took part in four Olympic Games, and today is recognized as one of the greatest athletes Canada has ever produced.

As the sixties progressed, there was a rekindled interest in organized women's hockey. By the seventies, leagues had been formed in Ontario, British Columbia, and the northeastern United States. University and varsity hockey also became more popular. In 1976, an enterprising former bullfighter named Charles Lewis tried to organize a professional ice hockey league, and set up headquarters in Tarzania, California. We have no record of the Women's Professional Ice Hockey League ever playing a game; but still, it was a good idea.

**CHA REGISTRATION —
FEMALE HOCKEY FOR
THE LAST 10 YEARS
(1987/88 TO 1996/97)**

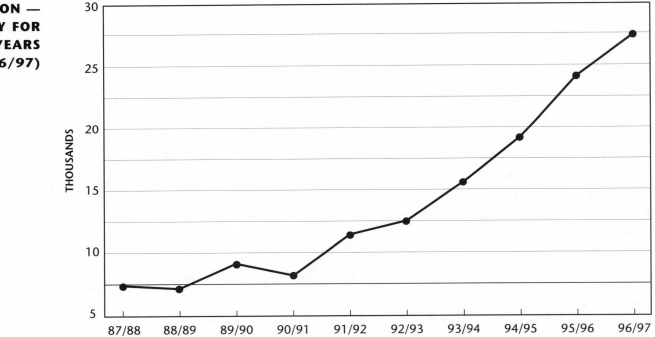

By the eighties, most people had accepted the idea of competitive, organized hockey teams for women. Over the past decade, registration for girls' hockey teams has skyrocketed: thirty thousand players were registered in women's hockey programs across North America in 1992. However, because of holes in the record-keeping system, both the Canadian Hockey Association (CHA) and USA Hockey believe this figure to be very conservative: the actual number of girls playing hockey in North America in 1992 was probably much higher than forty thousand. And this figure doesn't include those girls registered on mixed boys' teams.

In Canada, the 1992 CHA annual registration reports show an increase of almost one hundred percent from the previous year, with a total of almost fifteen thousand players registered. By 1997, the number reached thirty thousand. Today, Canadian officials estimate that registration in women's hockey has grown four hundred percent since the first Women's World Championships in 1990. Minor league hockey enrollment is up across the country, with the most significant increases in women's hockey. (See Figure 1 for the CHA's annual registration numbers for the past decade.)

The popularity explosion for women's hockey is partly due to the Women's World Championships. They were first held in 1990 in Ottawa; Canada won the gold medal, the United States won the silver, and Finland won the bronze. The second Women's World Championships, held in Finland in 1992, was a major event, and once again Canada captured the gold, with Team USA again winning the silver. The third Women's World Championships was held in Lake Placid, New York, in 1994, and once again, Canada beat Team USA (6–3) in the gold medal final. The first Pacific Rim Women's Hockey Championships, held in San Jose, California, in 1995, saw Canada, the United States, China, and Japan compete. Canada beat Team USA in a shoot-out after overtime to win the gold medal. In 1995 the Under-18 National Team were the first National Team in this age category to play in an international competition. The second Pacific Rim Women's Hockey Championships was held in Richmond, B.C. Canada won the gold, beating the U.S. The inaugural Three Nations Cup was held in Ottawa, with Canada, the United States, and Finland competing. It was a spectacular

Bev Mallory

Mickey Walker has been playing hockey since the 1930s, and has even played against the Preston Rivulettes.

show, and again Canada beat the U.S. in the gold medal final (1–0). The fourth Women's World Championships was held in Kitchener, Ontario, in 1997, and under a little more pressure from the American team, Canada persisted and earned a 4–3 win in overtime for the gold medal. The next scheduled Women's World Championships will take place in 1999 in Helsinki, Finland.

Women's hockey got the greatest boost, however, when it was added, for the first time, to the 1998 Winter Olympic Games in Nagano, Japan. Canada, the U.S., Finland, China, Sweden, and Japan were the six teams that competed. They were also the first, second, third, fourth, fifth, and sixth seeded teams, respectively, so it was no surprise when Finland, China, Sweden, and Japan placed accordingly. However, the big upset came when Canada couldn't rally in the final period of the final game. When Team USA won 3–1, they also won the first gold medal in Olympic women's hockey, settling a decade-long grudge against Canada, and beating their chief rival at their own game.

Women have also made an impression in the NHL. By now, we've all heard of Manon Rhéaume. She became a household name in the fall of 1991 after playing goal in a Junior A hockey game. She was the first Canadian woman to play hockey at that level. Later that year, Manon was invited to try out for the Tampa Bay Lightning of the NHL. Manon played a few exhibition games in the NHL, but decided to devote her time and energy to competing for the Canadian women's team going to Nagano, Japan.

Manon has two U.S. counterparts, Erin Whitten and Kelly Dyer. Erin Whitten, who was named All-American goaltender (three times), Eastern College Athletic Conference (ECAC) All-Conference goaltender (four times), and female athlete of the year (1994) by USA Hockey, was the first woman to play in a pro hockey game, to win a professional hockey game (Toledo Storm vs. Dayton), and to play a complete regulation professional game. Erin was also a member of the silver medal-winning Team USA from 1992 to 1998. Kelly Dyer is a four-time member of the U.S. Women's National Team (1990, 1992, 1994, and 1995), and she posted two wins for Team USA when she played on the 1995 U.S. Women's Select Team. She was top goaltender at the 1995 Pacific Rim Championships, with a zero goals-against average. Kelly is the third woman to play professional hockey, playing backstop against the Daytona Beach Sun Devils in 1994, as well as playing with the Louisville RiverFrogs, the West Palm Beach Blaze, and the Jacksonville Bullets.

Debbie Wright achieved another female first. In the same summer that Manon went to the Tampa Bay Lightning tryouts, Debbie was hired by the San Jose Sharks as a "scout." Scouts are people who search for talented young hockey players. Thanks to all this attention, women's hockey is one of the fastest-growing participation sports in North America. Women's hockey programs are now a recognized branch of both the CHA and USA Hockey, which ensure that every young player can enjoy the game of hockey, and that girls can play on mixed teams if they wish. But the CHA and USA Hockey encourage all-female teams, believing that girls and women are best served when they play with their peers. And in communities where there are enough female players, girls' teams and leagues are established. Why do girls sometimes choose to play on boys' teams? Well, I asked Justine Blainey that question. She was only thirteen when she took the Ontario Hockey Association to the Supreme Court of Ontario over the right to play hockey in a boys' league. Why? Justine wanted more competition and more ice time, and she wanted to play at a rink that was closer to home. "It was crazy. In the girls' league, I played once a week at a rink twenty miles away; while in the boys' league, my brothers played every other day, in our neighborhood, with far better players." Integration or segregation? For Justine, that was the issue at hand. She summed it up in one word — "checking."

"There's nothing wrong with checking if it's done properly. But there's a *no intentional body checking* rule in women's hockey, and that just means the players are trickier, and use other forms of checking you can't see. Some players, such as myself, prefer to play hockey with checking — the body contact can be exhilarating."

Justine won her case, and in the years since there have been many changes for women who play hockey. Women now have the option of playing either in a boys' league or in a girls' league. There have been many positive changes within the women's system itself. Women now have access to more ice time, better levels of competition, and the opportunity to progress to a high level of international play.

THE ONTARIO WOMEN'S HOCKEY ASSOCIATION

The Ontario Women's Hockey Association (OWHA) is a world leader in women's hockey. Through determination and effort, the OWHA has brought women's hockey to the World Championships and Olympic-level competition.

Founded in 1975, the OWHA oversees all ages and levels of competition in Ontario, including over four hundred girls' and women's teams with players ranging in age from four to seventy-four. In addition to the twenty-three categories of annual provincial championships, players can also participate in the Ontario Winter Games, the Canada Winter Games, and many exciting programs centered around competition, fun, and friendship. In 1982 the OWHA successfully organized and hosted the annual Canadian National Championships held in Brantford, Ontario. Inspired by the positive response, the OWHA then coordinated the first Women's World Hockey Tournament in 1987. Honorary Chairperson Hazel McCallion, mayor of Mississauga and a former hockey player, saw teams from Sweden, Switzerland, Japan, Holland, the United States, and Canada compete, while West Germany, China, Australia, Great Britain, and Norway sent official delegates.

PRO FILE

ABBY HOFFMAN

All-Round All-Star

Abby Hoffman made headlines across Canada in 1956 because she wanted to play hockey. In the end, the nine-year-old never got to finish her season. But Abby's love of sports continued; she turned her attention to track and field, eventually representing Canada in four Olympic Games. More recently, she served as director of Sport Canada, the governing body of amateur sports.

Why did young Abby want to play hockey when few other girls were playing? Abby thinks it's pretty simple. "My whole family was sports-oriented and athletic. I had two older brothers who played hockey, so it was easy for me to play with them. The tennis courts across the street doubled as an ice rink during the winter months. And most importantly, no one in my family ever said to me, a girl shouldn't play hockey."

Abby didn't see any other girls in the neighborhood playing hockey; it was mostly a boys' environment in those days. That didn't stop her. "I hated to be left behind, so I'd tag along and play any sports with the kids on my block." The decision to play in a league with her brothers seemed like a natural choice.

"When it was time for my brothers to join, I decided I wanted to play too. I saw an ad in the paper for a new league starting at the University of Toronto. I asked my parents to find out if girls could play. When my mother called, they said no. But we went down on registration day to see if there was a team I could play for."

While Abby's mother went to inquire somewhere, Abby stayed in the lineup. When she got to the front, she registered just like everyone else. "I didn't think I was doing anything wrong; I just wanted to play hockey. When I registered I showed my birth certificate for age confirmation, and no one bothered to look at my sex. In a few weeks the league called and said I had been assigned to a team. My parents were a little taken aback, but there was really no debate. I was on a team and I was going to show up." Abby cut her hair and went to the arena with all of her equipment on. She only had to lace up her skates at the rink. She called herself Ab Hoffman. The discovery of her true identity caused quite a controversy. "The question of girls playing hockey with boys hadn't even been asked yet, so it was not a matter of acceptance. It was a curiosity; people were incredulous. They couldn't believe it. Most people assumed that no girl would *want* to play."

Even though the attitudes and rules have changed since 1956, there are still people who don't think girls should play hockey. Abby believes this perception is wrong. "It's a great game for girls and it's Canada's national game. There's no reason why girls can't, or shouldn't, play hockey."

Abby's lifelong commitment to sports and to athletic excellence makes her a good role model for female athletes. We asked Abby what advice she would give to someone who wants to play hockey — or even make it to the Olympics. "I would encourage them to pursue their dream. Anything is possible if you try hard enough; you never know the outer limits of your capabilities."

PRO FILE

CHRISTA AND DANIELLE BULL

Sister Team Works

Linda Bull

Christa and Danielle Bull are sisters. And for the most part, they get along well. So it only seemed natural that when it came time to play hockey, they play on the same team. Christa, twelve, and Danielle, ten, both play for the Esquimalt Kiwanis, a junior girls' team in Victoria's Minor league hockey association.

They're still friends, but on the ice it's a different story. You see, Christa plays in goal, while Danielle plays out. They have great fun at practices, and Danielle especially enjoys it when she gets a breakaway and takes a shot on goal. Is Christa afraid of her sister's slap shot? "Not really, I just relax when I see her coming at me. She has a pretty weak shot right now. And just because she's younger doesn't mean I have to let her score."

Danielle practices every day, trying to improve her favorite shot, the wrist shot. "One day I'll surprise Christa. She won't even see the puck sailing right past her into the net."

Christa started in goal the usual way — their regular goaltender was sick. And it was the day they had a big tournament against a boys' team. Christa was the logical choice; she had played goal one other time, in practice. They won the game, and Christa's been playing in net ever since.

Christa finds goalie equipment heavier than the regular equipment, but she's used to it. And she reads *Behind the Mask* for goaltending points and positions. "I really want to win every game, so I try to stay calm, and I always watch the puck. When I'm focused, I find it's easier to keep the puck out of my net."

Christa went through many sports before deciding on hockey; her brother was playing and it sounded like fun. She likes to be active, and in hockey there's always something to do — drills, skating skills, and practicing glove saves. Christa has found her position, and she's planning to try out for the 2006 Olympic Team.

Danielle started playing hockey this year, and she wears most of her sister's old equipment. She chose hockey over baseball and figure skating because it sounded more exciting. "You can play hockey year-round, skate fast, stick-handle, and shoot the puck hard." Her favorite part of hockey is getting to take shots on goal. "I hit the puck extra hard when Christa's in the net. She doesn't say anything, her face says it all. She'll get me in the change room with the snow from her skates." Danielle thinks playing against a boys' team is pretty easy. "It's not hard work if you enjoy it."

CHAPTER 2

The Game of Women's Hockey

HOW IS IT PLAYED? WHAT ARE THE RULES?

Hockey is an easy game to understand. The object is simple: to shoot a small rubber disk, called a puck, into the opposing team's net. At the end of the game, the team with the most goals wins.

Most organized hockey games are played on a rink, a patch of ice surrounded by a barrier called "the boards." The boards are about three feet high; when the puck goes over them, play stops. The average rink is about two hundred feet long and eighty-five feet wide (see Figure 2), although in Europe it is a little wider, two hundred feet long by one hundred feet wide. This may help explain why Europeans are often better skaters — they're used to playing on a larger ice surface. The larger ice surface is used for all international competitions, including the Women's World Championships and the Olympic Games.

In hockey, two goals, called "nets," are at each end of the rink. Each net is four feet high and six feet wide. The marked-off area in front of the net is called the "crease."

In the old days, a hockey team could have as many as fifteen players on the ice at one time. By the 1920s, seven skaters was the standard. When the NHL first started in 1917, teams had six skaters — three forwards, two defensemen, and one "rover" — plus one goaltender. The goalie is a player who wears special equipment and "protects the net"; this means that she tries to stop the puck from going into the goal. She is the only player allowed to skate in the crease.

The days of the rover are long gone. These days, each team has a goalie and five skaters. The five skaters include three forwards — the center, the left wing, and the right wing — and two defense.

The standard hockey game is one to one and a half hours long, and consists of three "periods." Normally, games are "stop time," which means the timekeeper stops the clock when there is a break in the action. In women's hockey, and in minor or recreational leagues, the periods are almost always shorter and some may not have stop time.

Hockey games at all levels are presided over by on-ice officials. There are two kinds of officials: referees, who are in charge and may call penalties, and linesmen, who help the referees. All officials wear black-and-white striped sweaters. The referees are distinguished by a red band wrapped around each arm.

Several lines are painted on the rink. In the middle of the ice is a thick red line called, of course, the "red line." Closer to each net is a thick "blue line." The blue lines mark off the defensive zones.

In addition, five circles are painted on the ice, two in each team's end and one at center ice. These mark the areas where the referee drops the puck to begin play, and are called "face-off circles." They are named after the "face-off," which occurs when the two opposing centers try to gain control of the puck for their team, after it is dropped between them on the ice.

Hockey has lots of rules, most of which are designed to keep the players safe, or to keep the game moving. One important rule is the "offside." According to this rule, no offensive player can enter the defensive zone before the puck does. This simply means that nobody on your team can cross the other team's blue line until the puck has crossed that blue line. The referee will always be happy to remind you when you break this rule!

Another important rule to remember is "icing." Icing the puck means a player has shot the puck from her end of the rink down to the goal line of the

Figure 2
RINK

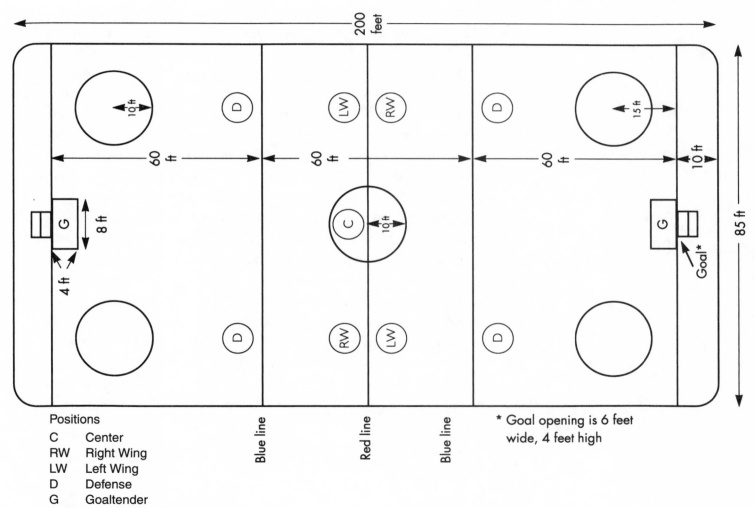

Positions
C   Center
RW   Right Wing
LW   Left Wing
D   Defense
G   Goaltender
Note the five face-off circles.

Blue line

Red line

Blue line

* Goal opening is 6 feet wide, 4 feet high

opposing team, and this usually causes the referee to blow her whistle and stop play. However, if the puck enters the net, icing won't be called and a goal is allowed.

Men's and women's hockey use the same rules and regulations, except for one important difference. No intentional body checking is allowed in women's hockey at any level, from recreational hockey right up to the World Championships. Body checking is when a player uses her hip or shoulder to slow or stop an opponent who has control of the puck. Players may use the body to "ride" another player off the puck, but direct and intentional checking is penalized. The no-check rule allows players to concentrate on the skills of hockey — skating, passing, stickhandling, and shooting. While the rule helps decrease the chance of injury and promotes fair play in a game where strength and size can dominate, it is still controversial. Many women feel body checking is an essential part of hockey, while some European teams would like to see body checking allowed during international and World Championship games. They believe this would inspire larger crowds and give women's hockey more credibility.

In North America, the CHA insists that it won't consider a rule change, and USA Hockey concurs. Some people feel that allowing body checking would make women's hockey more exciting. Purists fear that body checking would hurt the quality of the game, reducing it to one of size and not finesse. The body checking debate will certainly be around for a while.

BARBARA WILLIAMS

NHL Skating Coach

How does a figure skater figure in hockey? Just ask Barbara Williams. She's a former champion figure skater who teaches power skating to the pros. She was the first "recognized" female skating coach in the NHL, and the official skating coach of the New York Islanders in 1977.

"The players' skating style needed work," says Barbara, and she was quite surprised that they were so receptive to her coaching. Being female was a plus. "They didn't think a figure skater could help them play hockey. But in teaching them how to skate properly, I was really teaching them how to play better hockey."

Al Arbor, the Islanders' coach, saw what a great job she was doing and announced to the press that he had hired Barbara as the first female coach in the NHL. "That was big news in those days, a women directly involved in the NHL. It was an unbelievable time for me."

Barbara not only coached the Islanders, but went on to become the official skating coach for the New Jersey Devils, as well as four NHL farm teams. She is also the only woman to have her own hockey school in Long Island, New York. "I love helping kids of all ages, not only to be better skaters but to feel good about themselves."

Barbara Williams

PRO FILE

AUDREY BAKEWELL

Power Skating Coach to the Pros

Con Boland

Audrey Bakewell is another power skating instructor who has worked with the pros for over twenty years — the Calgary Flames, Edmonton Oilers, New York Rangers, and St. Louis Blues, to name a few. Audrey runs her own power skating schools, as well as intensive summer hockey camps, throughout North America and Europe. She also offers a girls' summer hockey camp, where she teaches the same skills to aspiring players as she would to professionals. "I've been involved with professional hockey for a long time, and if you are seriously interested in playing a top-level game, then you need to establish your skating skills base."

Power skating means many things. It is not just the ability to skate fast and hard; it also includes posture, agility, and control.

For more information regarding the Audrey Bakewell Power Skating School, you can reach Audrey at (403) 425-4193.

CHAPTER 3

All Dressed Up with Someplace to Go

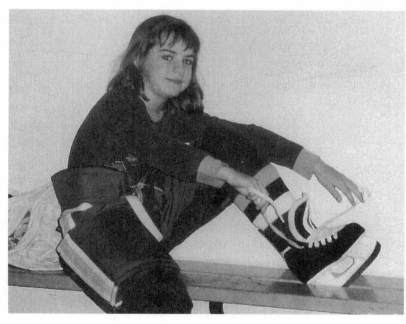

Barbara Stewart

DRESSED FOR SUCCESS

Hockey requires specialized equipment — skates and sticks for starters. It can be a very fast game, and even with the no intentional body checking rule, there is still a certain amount of body contact. The ice is hard, and if you get hit with the puck — ouch. You'll need to be well protected.

In this chapter, I'm going to look at all the different pieces of equipment that hockey players use. (In Chapter 5, I'll explain the special equipment that goaltenders wear.) I'll tell you what you need, how it works, and how much it costs. I'll help you get outfitted from head to toe. For a sneak preview, you might want to take a look at Figure 3, an illustration of a player dressed in full equipment.

IS THERE SPECIAL EQUIPMENT FOR WOMEN?

The quick answer is "yes." While most hockey equipment is designed for men, all sports companies realize the importance of properly fitting equipment, and most strive to meet the unique demands of the female player. Companies such as Nike, Canstar, Bauer, CCM, Louisville, and Daignault-Rolland produce hockey equipment in various styles for all sizes and shapes. Many companies have a special department that deals with women's concerns about equipment. Normally, equipment recommended for female players is designed and built specifically for the smaller, lighter player.

Louisville Hockey, a company that produces female protective gear, has met with such overwhelming success that it has expanded its women's line of

pro tip

- Reduce the risk of injury and improve your performance by choosing equipment designed to fit the female anatomy.

- Select shin guards that are narrower at the calf, pants that are shorter and slimmer at the waist, and shoulder pads that properly support and protect the bust.

hockey equipment to include several styles of hockey pants, gloves, shoulder pads, sticks (wood and composite), and replacement skate blades, all proportionately designed for the female athlete. Their TPS800 series has made Louisville the leader in female hockey equipment and sticks. Kelly Dyer, a former U.S. National Team member (1990–1995) who was nominated as 1998 Woman of the Year in Sports, is a product manager at Louisville Hockey. She contributes her expertise, knowledge, and valuable insight on the different sizes, playing styles, and positions used in women's hockey to help create the highest caliber female-specific protective gear and sticks available today. "Our goal is to provide performance advantages that will maximize playing potential, thus improving the game," Kelly explains.

A Canadian company called Daignault-Rolland — DR for short — produces a line of women's hockey equipment called Rage. The Rage series is designed for women; you have a better fit without compromising protection. The pants have narrower legs and a tapered hip, the gloves are designed with narrow palms and fingers. DR's Rage series offers two types of shoulder pads, elbow pads, shin pads, hockey pants, and gloves.

A WORD ABOUT BUYING EQUIPMENT

One of the drawbacks to playing hockey is the cost of equipment. You could easily spend $1000 to $2000 Cdn ($700 to $1400 U.S.) before you even step on the ice. The prices I'm going to list are approximate costs in Canadian and U.S. dollars. The first thing you should do before you make this kind of investment is to ask yourself: *Do I really like this game?* If you're uncertain at all, get the least expensive equipment — used equipment is often the best bargain — or borrow from a friend, a sister, or a brother. However, I can't emphasize enough how important it is to have properly fitting equipment, new or used, that offers suitable protection. Once you've made up your mind, take your time selecting equipment that's right for you. How do you know what's right? Well, I recommend you follow these three criteria:

1. *Protection:* Is it approved by the CSA or BNQ in Canada, or the HECC in the U.S.? Equipment that meets the rigorous safety standards of these organizations will be clearly marked. Remember, the more advanced your level of play, the more protection you'll need.

2. *Fit:* Don't be embarrassed to try on all your equipment in the store so that you can be assured of a proper fit. Put the gear on and move around. You want equipment that fits you now, not that you plan on growing into.

3. *Comfort:* Your equipment should feel comfortable. It shouldn't be bulky or cumbersome; it shouldn't pinch or cut off your circulation. Again, try everything on in the store; that's the only way to find out if it is comfortable or not.

3. Player dressed in full equipment

helmet

facial protector

throat protector

shoulder pads

gloves

elbow pads

hockey pants

shin pads

skates

stick

pro tip

EQUIPMENT CHECKLIST

1. Head
- ☐ helmet with chin strap
- ☐ facial protector
- ☐ throat protector

2. Arms, chest, and shoulders
- ☐ shoulder pads
- ☐ elbow pads
- ☐ gloves
- ☐ sports bra

3. Lower body
- ☐ pants
- ☐ pelvic protector
- ☐ shin pads
- ☐ hockey socks
- ☐ garter

4. Feet
- ☐ skates
- ☐ athletic socks

5. Other Equipment
- ☐ sticks
- ☐ tape
- ☐ equipment bag
- ☐ skate guards
- ☐ skate wipe

HEAD

- Helmet with chin strap
- Facial protector
- Throat protector

Helmet with Chin Strap

All players at every level of women's hockey must wear a specially designed helmet. These helmets must meet the safety requirements set out by the governing hockey organization in your country.

Ice hockey is a collision sport that can be dangerous; your helmet just might save you from serious injury one day. Do not use a helmet if the shell is cracked, or if the interior padding has deteriorated. Your helmet should be replaced if anything is broken, loose, worn down, or if screws are missing.

Make sure that your helmet does not slide or rotate around your head; it should fit snugly, without pinching. All nuts and screws should be flush and tight. Look for a mask that comes with a facial protector. And remember, keep your chin strap on and snapped in place when you play.

Used Helmets

A new helmet is not very expensive so, for health and safety reasons, I suggest you avoid used helmets.

Cost
Kids: $70 to $90 Cdn; $50 to $65 U.S.

Adult recreational: $60 Cdn and up; $35 U.S. and up

Adult competitive: $60 Cdn and up; $35 U.S. and up

Facial Protector

Hockey leagues require that you wear approved protection for your face as well as your head. There are two basic kinds of face protection: the "cage" and the "visor."

The cage is made of wire, and resembles a lightweight baseball catcher's mask. The "spider" cage is not approved for hockey by the CSA; it is used mainly for roller or street hockey. The visor is a clear plastic mask that looks as if it was designed for outer space. Both types of protection have relative advantages and disadvantages. The cage does not fog up, as visors sometimes do. On the other hand, because visors are clear, they offer better visibility overall.

The face mask should fit snugly around the bottom of your chin. Wear your mask around the house when you first get it so that you can adjust to seeing the world from behind the mask.

Used Face Masks

Used cages are okay if they are not cracked or dented; used visors are okay if they are not cracked or scratched. But, once again, new masks are inexpensive. You won't save a lot of money buying a used mask, so why take the chance?

Cost

All levels: $30 Cdn and up; $15 U.S. and up

---

pro tip

EQUIPMENT

- Wear all of your equipment all the time you are on the ice.

- Always dry your equipment after each use.

HELMETS

- If you have a narrow head, you may want to try a CCM helmet; if you have a rounder head, you may want to try a Cooper SK2000, in junior or senior sizes.

pro tip

FACE MASKS

- Buy special spray to prevent your visor fogging up. Ask for it at your sporting goods store. I think Itech is the best.

- The "spider cage" style mask is not CSA approved.

- Invest in a soft visor protector to use when the helmet is in your bag.

THROAT PROTECTORS

- Some players wear turtlenecks instead of a throat protector. Don't kid yourself; a shirt won't protect you from a dangerous cut.

Throat Protector

A throat protector is mandatory at all levels of women's hockey. As you know, skates are sharp and the ice is slippery. It's easy to fall on the ice, and a fallen player may be cut by a skate. A throat protector covers the part of your body most vulnerable to cuts. It's a very simple device, a pad that looks something like a headband and fits comfortably around your neck.

Used Throat Protectors

A used one is fine, provided it is still in good condition. But, once again, new ones are inexpensive. Cut corners somewhere else.

Cost

All levels: $20 to $40 Cdn; $12 to $25 U.S.

ARMS, CHEST, AND SHOULDERS

- Shoulder pads
- Elbow pads
- Gloves
- Sports bra

Shoulder Pads

Shoulder pads protect your shoulders, upper arms, collar bone, upper chest, and back. They should fit like a snug T-shirt — you don't want them falling off.

If finding the exact size is a problem, try going to a slightly bigger size. If they are a tad big but they cover all the areas properly and feel comfortable, that's the best protection you can get.

Try the shoulder pads on in the store, and make sure that they are fully flexible. A pair too small or too large will restrict movement. You should be able to get at least two years' use out of a good pair of shoulder pads, more if you've stopped growing. You should wear a sports bra underneath, as you would for any vigorous sports activity.

Used Shoulder Pads

There's nothing wrong with used shoulder pads as long as they are clean, fit well, and offer full protection. I find brand-new shoulder pads pricey, especially for the recreational player who has no interest in playing rough. A good pair of used pads is often the way to go, and will probably provide years of devoted service.

Some shoulder pads for women are made with formed "cups," as you see in women's bathing suits. They're bulky, but they provide the proper protection. Newer and better models are being designed and developed every day. Look for the one that's right for you.

Cost

Kids: $60 Cdn and up; $35 U.S. and up

Adult recreational: $75 to $250 Cdn; $45 to $150 U.S.

Adult competitive: $100 Cdn and up; $60 U.S. and up

pro tip

SHOULDER PADS

- If you're bigger chested, make sure you choose shoulder pads that are longer, to give you adequate coverage.

pro tip

ELBOW PADS

- A simple rule to avoid embarrassment in the change room: shoulder pads go on before elbow pads.

- Small women can use less expensive boys' or junior-sized elbow pads.

Elbow Pads

Guess what part of the body elbow pads cover? Don't worry, there's no trick here, except to find a pair of pads that fits well. It's important that they fit closely, so that when you play they don't move around. They should reach halfway down your forearm, between your wrist and elbow, and halfway up your biceps so that they protect the entire elbow joint. There should be no open area on your arm where you can get hit by the puck.

A fall on your elbow can really hurt, and there's nothing funny about damaging your humerus bone. Protecting your elbows means that you will also protect your shoulders and hands.

Used Elbow Pads

Yes! As long as they are clean and have all their straps attached.

Cost

Kids: $30 to $45 Cdn; $15 to $25 U.S.
Adults: $55 Cdn and up; $35 U.S. and up

Gloves

When you're looking for a pair of gloves, keep two points in mind: feel and comfort. When you try a glove on, you'll know if it fits right away. It'll feel like putting a baseball mitt on. When it's on, you should be able to feel the heel of your hand fit perfectly into the heel of the glove, while your fingers touch the end of the glove.

When looking for gloves, go through the entire selection and try them all on.

You shouldn't be able to feel the bones in the back of your hand through the glove padding. The gloves should provide exceptional protection, enough to absorb any shock.

Some players prefer to wear gloves that are looser, to give them better stick control. I don't recommend cut-off gloves because they can be dangerous to your unprotected wrists.

The palm of the glove will form to the shape of your hand. Synthetic materials have a tendency to "form," and stay that way. Leather gloves will return to their normal position, although the life expectancy of leather may be shorter. Palms should be soft and pliable, so that you can "feel" the puck on the end of your stick.

Used Gloves

Used gloves offer two advantages: they are less expensive, and they are already broken in. Used gloves made from synthetic materials, as opposed to leather, are the best bet since they have the longest life span.

Cost
Kids: $40 to $75 Cdn; $25 to $45 U.S.
Adult recreational: $70 to $100 Cdn; $40 to $60 U.S.
Adult competitive: $75 Cdn and up; $45 U.S. and up

Sports Bra
Cost
$30 Cdn and up; $15 U.S. and up

pro tip

GLOVES

- Gloves with leather palms give you a better feel and grip on your stick.

pro tip

HOCKEY PANTS

- Hang your hockey pants up to dry after every game or practice.

- Look for hockey pants specially designed for women.

LOWER BODY

- Pants
- Pelvic protector
- Shin pads
- Hockey socks
- Garter

Pants

There are two styles of hockey pants: the familiar old-style shorts and the two-piece style, often referred to as Cooperalls, a brand name that has become a generic term for this style of pant. Pants used to require suspenders, but most models made today do not.

The majority of players still use the old style of pant: a one-piece unit that reaches the top of the knee and has the padding built right in to protect your middle section, lower back, kidneys, backside, hips, and upper thighs.

With the Cooperalls, a padded girdle is worn underneath the unpadded nylon pants. Many players prefer the padded girdle and feel this style is more comfortable. It's just a matter of taste.

Used Pants

Hockey pants are another item I find pricey, so you can save some money if you're able to pick up a good pair of used pants. Make sure they're clean, without rips or tears, and that all the padding is in place. Check to see if they require suspenders; suspenders, which are sometimes called "bachelor buttons," can be bought at most hockey supply stores for around $20 Cdn and $12 U.S.

Cost

Kids: $70 Cdn; $40 U.S.

Adult recreational: $90 to $150 Cdn; $55 to $90 U.S.

Adult competitive: $150 Cdn and up; $90 U.S. and up

Pelvic Protector

A pelvic protector or "jill" is a triangular piece of equipment that protects the pelvic area. There is one common design that is comfortable and fits according to waist size. Sometimes after a hard season the waistband will lose some of its elasticity and stretch, becoming loose, so make sure the waistband is made of good quality elastic.

Used Pelvic Protectors

Um… no thanks.

Cost

All levels: $20 to $35 Cdn; $15 to $20 U.S.

Shin Pads

Shin pads provide protection to your lower legs and knees. Too big? They'll slide out of position. Too small? Your shins and knees will be left exposed and won't have enough protection. You also don't want the pad to go down too low, because it will get jammed in your skate. The bottom of your hockey pants should overlap the top of your shin pads.

Shin pads are held in position with Velcro straps and tape. Velcro is reusable, so I only use tape over my socks. Don't forget that your hockey socks ($10–$20)

pro tip

SHIN PADS

• Since most regular shin pads are wider and made for men's legs, many recreational female players will use junior-sized shin pads.

cover your shin pads; make sure that your shin pads are in the proper position, then pull up your socks. A hockey garter ($10 Cdn; $5 U.S.) will ensure that your socks stay in place!

Used Shin Pads

You can quite often find good shin pads at the used sporting goods store. Make sure that the pads aren't cracked, the padding isn't worn thin, and that the foam or cloth lining is still in place.

Cost

Kids: $60 to $90 Cdn; $35 to $55 U.S.
Adult recreational: $90 Cdn; $55 U.S.
Adult competitive: $90 Cdn and up; $55 U.S. and up

FEET

- Skates
- Athletic socks

Skates

Skates are the most important part of a player's equipment, so spend time looking for a pair that you'll be happy with. The key to skates is *fit*. If they don't fit properly, they won't perform. Skates also provide protection for the foot and the Achilles tendon.

The skate should fit snugly, with your toes just touching the end of the boot. When it comes to width, skates should be as tight as possible, without painful pinching. Ask the clerk at the sports store to help you find a pair that fits perfectly.

There are three kinds of skate boots: leather, nylon, and molded plastic. For the recreational hockey player, molded skates are fine. They are generally lower in price, and if you have a problem with your foot, such as a bone spur or a callus, molded skates are very comfortable. Serious hockey players normally wear skates with a sewn boot, made either of leather or nylon. These offer better protection, and mold to the shape of your foot for better control.

Skate Sharpening

You can get your skates sharpened at any sports store that sells skates, or at your local arena. How often you sharpen your skates depends on how often you use them. A good blade will hold a sharp edge for at least five to ten uses. Remember to completely dry your boot and blade after each use, to prevent rust from forming and to ensure longer wear.

A deep groove or hollow in your blade means a sharper edge — enabling quicker turns. If you play defense you may want to consider a deeper groove because of all the sharp, fast turns you will have to make. The skate blade may also be "rockered" — sharpened so that the ends of the blades are curved up, once again allowing for more movement and quicker changes of direction.

Forwards and centers prefer a shallow groove or hollow. They rely more on speed to get them from one end of the rink to the other, so a blade that promotes gliding is best.

pro tip

SKATES

- Use wax laces to help keep your skates well fastened.

- Don't wrap the laces around your ankle; this could cut off circulation to your foot.

- Always dry your skate blades after each use so that they don't rust.

- Don't wear heavy socks or an extra pair; one thin, warm pair of socks is fine — the less material there is between your foot and the skate boot, the more control you will have.

Used Skates

Used skates are much less expensive than new ones, but they have a disadvantage — they have already been broken in to the shape of the previous owner's foot.

Cost

Kids: $100 to $160 Cdn; $60 to $95 U.S.

Adult recreational: $80 to $200 Cdn; $50 to $120 U.S.

Adult competitive: $200 Cdn and up; $120 U.S. and up

Athletic Socks

Cost

$5 to $8 Cdn; $3 to $5 U.S.

OTHER EQUIPMENT

- Sticks
- Tape
- Equipment bag
- Skate guards
- Skate wipe

Sticks

Sticks are hard to choose by sight: you just have to go through the rack in the store and pick out one that feels right for you. When you're trying out a stick be sure to stand up on your toes. This will give you the same pitch and height as wearing your hockey skates.

One thing to check is the "lie" of the stick. This is the angle where the blade meets the shaft. Every stick has its lie marked on it. A low lie (three or four) puts the blade, and therefore the puck, away from your feet. A high lie (seven) brings the blade and the puck closer to your feet. For starters, try a stick with a five or six lie.

How long should your stick be? To find out, place the end of the blade on the ice between your skates, with the shaft straight up in front of your body. The top of the stick should reach somewhere between your chest and the tip of your nose. If it's too long, don't worry; any sports store will gladly cut the stick to your personal specifications.

One more thing. Sticks come with left- or right-handed curves, and sometimes with no curves at all. It can be confusing, but remember that the type of curve has nothing to do with whether you are left- or right-handed. It has to do with how you shoot (left or right) and with what feels most comfortable to you.

Used Sticks

Forget it! Unless it was your brother's or your sister's, and you know it isn't cracked or broken.

Cost

Kids: $10 to $40 Cdn; $5 to $25 U.S.

Adult recreational: $30 to $50 Cdn; $15 to $30 U.S.

Adult competitive: $30 Cdn and up; $15 U.S. and up

pro tip

STICKS

- Taping saves wear on the blade and provides a better (stickier) surface for controlling the puck.

- A knob or bulge of tape at the end of the shaft helps keep the stick from sliding out of your hands. It also makes it easier to pick up your stick when you've dropped it on the ice.

- Always bring two sticks to a game; one might break.

- Write your name on your stick with a marker.

Tape

Cost

$3 to $5 Cdn; $2 to $3 U.S.

Equipment Bag

Cost

Kids: $45 Cdn; $25 U.S.

Adults: $50 Cdn; $30 U.S.

Skate Guards

Cost

$10 Cdn; $5 U.S.

ANGELA JAMES

Wayne Who?

Angela James is one of the superstars of women's hockey. She holds dozens of league scoring records and has been a powerhouse in leading Canada's National Team to gold medals in four World Championships, two Pacific Rim Championships and two Three Nations Cups. She's so good, in fact, she's often called "The Wayne Gretzky of Women's Hockey." It's a nickname, however, Angela says she could do without. "Although it's a nice honor, I'd just like to be known as the Angela James of female hockey, period."

Angela grew up the youngest of five children in Toronto. She started playing hockey at age eight, and discovered that she was better than most of the boys on her team; she won scoring trophy after scoring trophy. "The boys weren't too excited about that. They loved it when we won games, but not when they didn't win the awards."

Problems started after Angela's first season. Some of the other kids' parents were upset because Angela was such a good player — she intimidated a lot of the boys. Soon afterward, Angela moved to a girls' team and continued her illustrious hockey career in the female system.

When she finished high school, Angela enrolled at Seneca College in Toronto. She quickly became an integral member of the women's hockey team. She's still at Seneca today, but now she's a recreation coordinator and is responsible for organizing all of Seneca's intramural activities.

Hockey has always been an essential part of Angela's life, and she plans on keeping it that way. She works out every day to stay in top-notch shape. She runs three times a week, and still finds time to referee, play, coach, and instruct. She's also qualified to teach power skating and hockey skills.

When Angela played in Finland during the 1992 Women's World Championships, she really enjoyed the travel, and the thrill of the game. "Playing overseas

Courtesy National Women's Team Fact Book

was wonderful, the change and challenge of adapting to everything new and different. After we won, I stayed in Europe with a couple of teammates and traveled a bit. We ended up flying home on the same flight as the Canadian men's hockey team; they had just lost a tournament in Czechoslovakia. Together we reminisced about our games and our travels."

With her continuing commitment to hockey and to the development of the sport's young players, Angela James truly is a superstar.

You can catch her teaching with Breakaway Sports Consultants Inc., located at Seneca College and specializing in the development of adult hockey players. Her school offers classes for beginners, intermediate, and advanced players. For more information call (416) 494-5545.

Stephanie Boyd was simply continuing a family tradition when she took up hockey before she was four years old. "Hockey is a tradition in my family; everyone plays."

Stephanie started her hockey career in Gravenhurst, Ontario, and when she moved to Toronto, she played for the University of Toronto Varsity Blues and the Toronto Aeros. She had an opportunity to play hockey for Yale University on a scholarship, but decided to stay in Canada. "I loved playing with the Aeros and for the university. I enjoyed being busy with hockey and school."

During the summer months, Stephanie is in charge of a hockey camp for girls in Gravenhurst. Stephanie's hockey school has been running since 1990, and has been a huge success. "The school has expanded to a two-week session with on-ice and off-ice training. We teach the fundamental skills and basic concepts of the game. We like to make the experience at the school fun for the participants and the staff."

What makes Stephanie such a great player? Ask anyone: she's known around town for her "soft hands." "That's true. I have soft hands when I control the puck. My dad taught me how to stickhandle when I was just learning how to skate. Many players tend to hang on to their stick very tightly; I use a loose grip. When I take a pass or a shot, it's always very smooth. I can actually feel the puck when it leaves my stick."

Stephanie has dual citizenship, both Canadian and American. While many of her team members from both the University of Toronto Varsity Blues and the Toronto Aeros went on to become Canadian National Team players, Stephanie played for Team USA. It was funny to be playing against many of her friends, she said, but it also gave her an insider's advantage, since she knew all their plays.

STEPHANIE BOYD

Hot Shots and Cool Passes

Paul Sprunt

Stephanie was a member of Team USA for three years; in 1993 she won a gold medal at the Olympic Festival in San Antonio, Texas, and 1994 and 1995 saw two silver wins at the World Championships in Lake Placid, New York, and the Pacific Rim Championships in San Jose, California, respectively. Right now, she plays with the Mississauga Chiefs, a Senior AAA team, and continues to teach the game she loves.

Stephanie has the perfect job: she's a sales associate at Nike Canada Inc. She manages Nike accounts in the northern and eastern regions of Ontario for hockey, roller hockey, performance equipment, vision, and timing.

Stephanie believes that hockey can help a person grow and develop. "As we grow up, it's sometimes hard to deal with all of life's ups and downs. Sports can help you adjust and adapt to different situations, to understand what's important. A hockey team provides you with friends, support, and encouragement to grow as a person."

For more information on Stephanie Boyd's Female Hockey School, call (416) 321-9759.

CHAPTER 4

The ABCs of
Ice Hockey

SKATING, STICKHANDLING, PASSING, AND SHOOTING

The four basic skills you need to play hockey are skating, stickhandling, passing, and shooting. To keep things simple, I'll explain these skills in just enough detail to get you off and running.

There are two important points to remember. First, you can't learn how to play hockey simply by reading a book — at some point, you're going to have to go out on the ice and give it a try. Second, everyone has to start somewhere. Don't be embarrassed if you can't skate backward or can't flip the puck — the only way to learn and to improve is by practicing.

SKATING

Skating is the most important part of the game. If you want to excel at hockey, you must become a confident skater.

When you skate, you literally glide over the ice. As you push your blade across the frozen surface, the friction causes the blade to warm up and melt the ice for a moment — just long enough for you to glide. That's why it's sometimes more difficult to skate when it's very cold and the ice is harder than usual. You should become familiar with the following six elements of skating:

1. Stance
2. Skating forward
3. Edges

4. Stopping
5. Skating backward
6. Turning

4. Player in ready stance

Stance

"Stance" refers to the way you hold your body in ready position. (See Figure 4 for an illustration.) The proper stance gives you a firm foundation on which to build your skating technique; it should allow you to move easily in any direction. Just keep in mind these three points:

1. Bend your knees slightly.
2. Lean forward a little at the waist.
3. Keep your head up, eyes looking ahead, and concentrate on putting your body weight on the middle and back of each foot.

Maintain this basic stance all the time you are on the ice — whether you are skating forward or backward, turning or stopping. You can hold your stick with one or both hands, but keep it flat on the ice.

Comfort is the key to great skating. If you feel uncomfortable on your skates, you are probably leaning too far forward at the waist, or your knees may be too straight. It's natural to lean forward in an effort to keep your balance. Instead, though, bend your knees a little. By bending your knees, you are lowering your center of gravity, and this allows you to maintain the proper balance, power, and control.

Skating Forward

Push — glide. Push — glide. Push — glide. This is the basic rhythm to skating forward. You push with one foot, then glide on the other, over and over again. *Push — glide.* When you push, you actually push off to the side, with your forward knee bent and your pushing leg extended. Use long strokes for a relaxed glide, or short strokes for a speedier glide.

Skating Forward Tips

1. Stand comfortably in ready position, with your weight distributed evenly over the skate blades.
2. Push off to the side, with your forward knee bent and your pushing leg extended. Use your skate edge for pushing off.
3. Repeat, with your push-off foot now becoming your glide foot.

inside edge   outside edge   **5. Edges**

6. Stopping with both feet

Edges

Know your edges! Learning and mastering edges is an art, so don't get discouraged if it doesn't come naturally. Many professional hockey players haven't learned theirs yet. Control of your edges will come with experience and practice.

The skate has two edges: the inside edge and the outside edge. The inside edge is used mainly for pushing off, while the outside edge is used primarily for turning and stopping. (See Figure 5 for an illustration.)

Stopping

There are several ways you can stop on the ice. My least favorite is running into the boards! Most of us learn to stop a little bit at a time, as our confidence builds. So don't worry if you're a little apprehensive at first. It's natural.

"Stopping with both feet" is the easiest method for beginners. It also looks great! We've all seen hockey stars screech to a stop with both skates turned sideways, sending up a spray of ice.

When stopping with both feet, it is important to maintain your basic stance. But as you are skating, lean back slightly with your weight evenly distributed over both feet. Then, abruptly turn both skates at right angles to your skating direction, causing the blades to "plow" or "skid" against the ice. (See Figure 6 for an illustration of this stopping technique.)

When you stop with both feet, your feet should be close together, but still feel comfortable. In the beginning, aim for having your feet shoulder-width apart. As you practice and improve this stopping method, you'll be able to do it with your skates closer together.

Stopping Tips
1. Lean back a little, but keep your weight evenly distributed over both feet.
2. Quickly turn both skates perpendicular to your skating direction; keep your skates shoulder-width apart and your knees bent.
3. Dig in with your skate edges to help you stop.

SKATING BACKWARD

You have to adjust your stance slightly in order to skate backward. Your weight should be less centered and more over the ball of each foot. Bend your knees and crouch closer to the ice.

The strides in skating backward are the same as in skating forward; push off to the side, and then transfer your weight from the push-off foot to the glide foot. Keep your head up and, if you have a stick, extend it in front of you with the blade on the ice, not for support but to help maintain balance. Pretend you are about to sit down in a chair; this should give you the correct position. (See Figure 7 for an illustration of this technique.)

The more you practice skating backward, the more your skating forward will improve. Why? Because more balance is required to skate backward.

7. Skating backward

Skating Backward Tips
1. Bend your knees and lean forward slightly, with your weight over the ball of each foot. Keep one hand on your stick for better balance.
2. Push off to the side, using the skate edge. Extend your leg from the hip to maximize the push and strength of your entire leg.

3. Transfer your weight from the push-off foot to the glide foot. Repeat.
4. Don't wiggle your bottom; keep your head up and your shoulders level.
5. Use your stomach muscles to keep your back strong and erect.

Turning

There are two kinds of turns: the "glide" turn and the "crossover" turn.

The glide turn is the easiest. The very first time you lace on a pair of skates you will probably be able to do a glide turn. All you do is put your weight on your inside foot, and turn that foot in the direction you want to go. For example, if you want to turn right, put your weight on your inside (right) foot and turn it slightly to the right. Your inside foot should also be your lead foot. So if you want to turn left, put your weight on your lead foot (inside, or left) and turn it slightly to the left. Remember to lean into the turn.

Glide Turn Tips

1. Bend your knees and put your weight over your inside (lead) foot.
2. Turn the inside foot in the direction you want to go; the outside foot should be parallel but slightly behind.
3. The inside knee should bend further as the outside leg pushes off.

The crossover turn is more difficult to master than the glide turn, but it looks much cooler. In the crossover turn, your outside foot lifts over your inside foot as you continue skating. The crossover gives you more power and speed as you turn. You should begin a crossover turn by turning your body. With your shoulders parallel, slowly turn your hips. Keep your knees bent and your weight balanced

8. Crossover turn

on your inside foot. Your outside leg should come from behind, and as you lift it from the ice, push off with your edge to start the turn. As you cross over the outside leg, plant it on the ice in front of your inside leg. (See Figure 8 for an illustration.)

Crossover Turn Tips

1. Begin the turn by slowly turning your body.
2. Keep your knees bent, with your weight over the inside foot.
3. Push off with the outside leg and lift it to cross over in front of the inside leg.

9. Stickhandling

STICKHANDLING

Have you ever seen this happen in a hockey game? One player picks up the puck from behind her own net, then weaves and bobs her way all the way down to the other end of the ice to score. It's exciting to watch and shows you how valuable a good stickhandler can be to her team.

Now, not every player has the skill to stickhandle around her opponents from one end of the ice to the other — that takes years of practice. But you can quickly become a good stickhandler. All you have to do is remember the basic skills and techniques.

When stickhandling, put one hand at the very top of the shaft of your stick, and the other approximately eight to fourteen inches lower. If this feels awkward at first, don't worry; it will soon feel natural when you are skating down the ice carrying the puck.

If you are a right-handed shooter, then your left hand is the upper hand, and your right hand is the lower hand. If you are a left-handed shooter, then your right hand is the upper hand, and your left hand is the lower hand. The lower hand controls the stick and is the power behind the shots. Hold the stick with your fingers wrapped around the shaft, not with the butt in the palm of your hand. An important rule: keep your thumb out of the way. You can injure it if you don't keep it wrapped around the stick.

As you stickhandle, your arms should move in front of your chest, creating a weaving motion from side to side. This mainstay of stickhandling lets you move the puck away from an opponent on either side of you, until you can safely pass or skate away. (See Figure 9 for an illustration.)

Another thing to remember when you are skating with a stick and a puck is to never look directly down at the puck. Always keep your eyes trained ahead. By this I mean you should use a "split-vision" technique. By training your eyes ahead you should be able to see not only the puck as you carry it, but the rest of the rink, the players, and everything in front of you.

You can practice stickhandling any time; you don't even need to be on the ice. Many of hockey's greatest stickhandlers say that they spent hours in the driveway with a tennis ball honing their skills.

Stickhandling Tips

1. Keep your head up and your eyes looking ahead.
2. Keep the puck in front of you, on the back half of your blade.
3. Make sure that your arms and shoulders are relaxed as you move the puck back and forth.

PASSING

Making a Pass

It's true: the players who score goals get all the glory in hockey. But where would these snipers be if they didn't have someone passing the puck to them?

Passing is one of the finest arts in the game of hockey. Unfortunately, most players spend most of their time practicing shooting. It doesn't make sense. In a game, you might get four or five shots on the net, but you'll have to pass the puck as many as twenty to thirty times. What am I saying? Don't forget to practice passing!

It's easy to pass the puck; you simply push it toward the target with the blade of your stick. You should put enough power behind the puck to ensure that it reaches its target, your teammate's stick. But it's also important not to pass the puck too fast or too hard, because then the receiver can't control it.

Remember to aim first, then follow through. On the follow-through, the blade should not leave the ice too much, no more than a few inches. If your follow-through ends up looking like a golf swing, you could receive a penalty for high-sticking.

Practice passing by skating down the ice with a friend, moving the puck back and forth between you. You can also practice passing off-ice, using a tennis ball instead of a puck.

Passing Tips

1. Keep your head up and your eyes looking ahead and aimed at the target.
2. Push the puck toward your target.
3. Follow through; but remember, don't exaggerate this motion — the blade of your stick should only be a few inches above the ice.

Receiving a Pass

You're open, waiting for the pass, and your stick is ready for the puck. The puck comes sailing right toward your stick, a beautiful pass. You eagerly await your chance to make the big goal and win the game. The puck hits the blade of your stick and... bounces onto your opponent's stick. What went wrong?

You didn't "give." When you receive a pass, you have to allow for the puck's speed. It's like catching a moving object; your stick needs to absorb the impact.

To give when receiving a pass, move your stick slightly backward in the same direction the puck is moving, cup the blade (lean your top half toward the puck), and "catch" the puck with your stick.

Your stick should be "soft" (held loosely) when receiving, and "firm" (held more tightly) when passing or shooting. On both moves, the hand position should stay the same. (See Figure 10 for an illustration of two players passing and receiving.)

10. Two players passing and receiving.

Receiving Tips

1. Your stick must be on the ice — to give the passer a target.
2. Let your stick give a little.
3. Try to keep the blade of your stick steady and perpendicular to the pass.

SHOOTING

Coaches, parents, fans, and scouts will always notice you out there on the ice if you're a team player — one who plays with a positive attitude of participation and contribution. But to win the game you'll need to score a goal or two. In this section, I'm going to show you how to do all the major kinds of shots. These include:

1. Wrist shot
2. Backhand shot
3. Snap shot
4. Flip shot
5. Slap shot

It's important to realize that some of these shots are also valuable passing techniques; they should not be reserved for shots on net. As usual, there's one secret to good shots. That's right: the infamous "P" word, "practice."

Wrist Shot

The easiest shot to master is the wrist shot. As the name suggests, this shot is made with a snapping action of the wrist.

To make a wrist shot, assume your normal stance and hand position, with your hands about ten to fourteen inches apart on the shaft. Maneuver the puck to your shooting side, slightly behind your skates, with the puck in the middle of the blade of your stick.

Lean into the shot. As you do so, both wrists should turn in a quick motion.

11. Wrist shot

You should concentrate on turning them at the same time. The lower wrist should turn upward, with the back of the hand facing the ice. The upper wrist should turn downward, with the palm of the hand facing the ice. As you shoot, transfer your weight from your back foot to your front foot. This helps to pack power into your shot, as well as leaving you balanced and ready to play.

Keep your eyes on the target. You can glance down for a moment to make sure the puck is in the proper position, but remember to look back up at the target. Follow through as you make the shot. The height of your stick on the follow-through will influence the flight of the puck — the higher the stick, the higher the puck. But remember to avoid high-sticking. (See Figure 11 for an illustration of the wrist shot.)

12. Backhand shot

Wrist Shot Tips

1. Maneuver the puck to your shooting side and position it slightly behind your skates; keep your head up with your eyes on the target.

2. As you shoot, snap your wrists, and transfer your weight from your back foot to your front foot.

3. Follow through as you make the shot.

pro tip

HOCKEY SHOOTING TIPS

These tips were developed by Andria Hunter and former Toronto Maple Leaf Ron Ellis.

1. Forehand Wrist Shot

- Remember to transfer your weight from your back foot to your front foot as you move the puck forward.
- A low or high follow-through will determine how low or high the puck goes.
- When you finish your follow-through, your stick should always be pointing to your target.

2. Backhand Wrist Shot

- Do not have the puck too far in front of you when you set up this shot.
- Lean into the shot and bend your knees to raise the puck off the ice.

Backhand Shot

Goaltenders hate backhand shots because it is difficult to anticipate the direction of the puck. This gives you a better chance of scoring.

The backhand shot is similar to the wrist shot, except the puck is on the other side of the blade — the back instead of the front. The hand positions are identical, although lowering the bottom hand may give you more control. Try not to flip the puck through the air, but lean into the shot and shoot it hard and low. (See Figure 12 for an illustration.)

Backhand Shot Tips

1. Put the puck on the back of the blade of your stick. Keep your head and eyes up, with the puck behind your skates.
2. Snap your wrists and transfer your weight as you lean into the shot.
3. Follow through with control.

Snap Shot

The snap shot *snaps* the puck more than the wrist shot. The idea is to use the quick snapping action of the wrist to propel the puck.

Prepare for a wrist shot, hands ten to fourteen inches apart, but with the puck more toward the front of your skates. Swing your stick two feet back, then forward, down and hard, hitting the ice just behind the puck. Snap your wrists with a sharp turn.

This shot can be hard on your wrists, so make sure they feel strong enough to control the follow-through. Again, watch that your stick is kept low after the shot.

13. Flip Shot

3. Backhand Off a Deke

- Having a good backhand shot can be very useful in deking. (Deking is when you fake a shot to outsmart your opponent.)

- To shield the puck from another player, bring it close to your body.

- Dig your skates in and let a backhand wrist shot go at the net.

4. Snap Shot

- This is an effective quick-release shot.

- Use it when the puck comes to you from the corner and you can get a quick shot to the far side of the net. Since the goalie will be on the opposite side, you'll have a very good chance of scoring.

5. Practice, practice, practice!

Snap Shot Tips

1. Prepare the puck, and position it slightly in front of your skates.

2. Swing your stick down hard, hitting the ice just behind the puck; as you snap your wrists, transfer your weight from your back foot to your front foot.

3. Follow through with control and try to avoid swinging your stick too high.

Flip Shot

The flip shot is especially effective when the goaltender has fallen, dropped, or is sprawled in the crease. All you have to do is flip the puck over her into the net.

Flip shots also help you to aim for the corners of the net. It's easy for a goaltender to block a shot that's coming right toward her, but a shot aimed at one of the corners can deceive and outwit even the smartest and shrewdest goaltender.

The puck should be flipped using the front, or toe, of your stick's blade. Use the same hand position as the wrist shot, with your hands ten to fourteen inches apart, and put the blade in an "open" position. An open blade is the opposite of a cupped blade; the open blade should lean away from the puck as you take the shot. Flip the puck up in the air with a quick, sharp turn of the wrists. The open blade should catch on the back edge of the puck, causing it to flip or lift off the ice. (See Figure 13 for an illustration.)

Flip Shot Tips

1. Ready the puck with the blade of your stick in an open position.
2. Flip your wrists while lifting the puck off the ice.
3. Follow through so that the puck is flipped up through the air.

Slap Shot

In real life, the slap shot is never as easy, or even as fast, as it seems on television. The pros on TV have been perfecting their slap shots for many, many years. It will take you just as long to develop yours. While I don't recommend

14. Slap Shot

using a slap shot right away, I know it will be hard to resist the chance to practice. But remember: besides being the most difficult shot to master, the slap shot is also the hardest to control.

The backswing is the key to a good slap shot. Although it looks a little like a baseball swing, don't think that because you hit the game-winning home run last summer you can score the game-winning goal with the same swing. It won't work.

Start by bringing your stick back and up, and by sliding your lower hand about eight inches below its normal position. The stick should not be raised higher than your hips. Get ready to transfer your weight to your front foot as you prepare for your downstroke. Swing down and forward with your eyes on the puck, and hit the ice hard just behind the puck. For more impact, lean into the swing with your upper body. Follow through, keeping your stick tight and in control.

Because this shot takes more time to complete, be wary of other players skating up behind you. Once you have completed your swing, make sure you are evenly balanced. (See Figure 14 for an illustration of the slap shot.)

Slap Shot Tips

1. Raise your stick in a backswing with your lower hand sliding down the shaft. Place your weight on your back foot.
2. Transfer your weight to your front foot as you begin to swing downward.
3. Hit the ice and the puck hard, and follow through with a secure stance.

POSITIONS

Decisions, decisions. Once you decide to play hockey, you have to make another choice: What position should you play? All of the positions are fun, fast, and fairly easy to learn. So if you can't decide right away, just keep trying out the different spots. You'll know where you feel most comfortable. There are four basic positions to choose from: center, wing, defense, and goal.

After experimenting with different positions, most players settle into one that suits them best; however, a few players continue to alternate positions throughout their careers. There's a famous story about King Clancy, who played in the NHL years ago. In one game, because of injuries and penalties, Clancy played every position, including goal!

Center

The center plays in the middle of the forward line. She must be a good passer and stickhandler, a fast skater, and able to win face-offs.

Wing

There are two wingers on each forward line — the "left wing" and the "right wing" — who play on opposite sides of the center. Wingers often have good shots, are fast skaters, and don't mind going into the corners to dig out the puck.

Defense

There are two defense players on the ice during regular play. Their main job is to help prevent the other team from scoring, although they also help the forward line whenever they can. Defenders need to be strong skaters, both forward and backward, and must be able to keep their cool when the heat is on.

Goal

Goaltenders are unique players. A goalie must stay close to her net at all times, and must try to prevent the puck from entering it. Goalies wear equipment that is different from that of other players, and use a special kind of stick and skates. You have to have composure, nerve, and concentration to play goal.

PRO FILE

MARG McADAM

Ringette Ringer

Marg McAdam

Ringette is similar to hockey — there's skating, passing, shooting, and scoring — but a rubber ring is used instead of a puck and the stick is a cut-off hockey stick; that is, the blade is cut off. Ringette is very popular, although many players have made the transition to hockey. Marg McAdam is one such player. She began playing ringette when she was seven years old. Now she's a hockey All-Star, playing for the London Devilettes Senior AA team, out of London, Ontario.

Marg signed up to play ringette after her father saw an ad in the paper for a new game for girls. She ended up playing for twelve years, and was a ringette All-Star by the time she was nine. Ringette tournaments were held every weekend and Marg lived for the excitement and competition. But when she reached her teens, she lost interest. "It interfered with my social life. But then I found I missed the thrill of a competitive game. So I decided to play shinny hockey at the urging of a friend who played Junior A hockey. I enjoyed shinny so much, I was hooked; I started skating and playing hockey whenever and wherever I could."

Marg was elated when her university started a women's house league. This led to a tryout with the Kitchener-Guelph Snowhawks, one of the top women's teams in Ontario. Her tryout was a success, and she's been playing hockey ever since. "One of the biggest adjustments was the equipment; there's very little of it in ringette. And the most important difference was keeping my head up! In ringette, you don't have to look down at the ring on your stick, but in hockey you really have to pay attention."

Having played ringette had its advantages, Marg believes. For starters, it helped her develop a great wrist shot. "That's my secret weapon against my opponents. It's important to maintain your balance in a proper wrist shot. I wear my gloves a little shorter to give me good wrist movement. But I don't scrimp on padding." And her years of skating didn't hurt either. "My skating ability is definitely my biggest asset. Skating is so vital to hockey; if you can skate, you can play hockey."

So, for now, Marg is very busy playing Senior AA hockey, with a fantastic coach, Sue Scherer, a former National Team member.

PRO FILE

SUE
SCHERER

Sue Scherer

Sue Scherer is a two-time gold medal–winning former National Team member. She played during the inaugural 1990 World Championships in Ottawa, and at the 1992 World Championships in Tampere, Finland. It only seemed natural that her career would bring her back to coaching. "I have combined coaching and playing since I was fifteen years old, although most of my time now is spent coaching and teaching players and coaches the skills necessary to make hockey fun for everyone."

Before Sue became coach of the London Devilettes Senior AA team, the largest girls' and women's hockey association in the world, she coached everyone from a minor league boys' team in New Hamburg, a town just outside of London, to varsity women. Sue was head coach for the Guelph Gryphons, the university women's varsity team, from 1993 to 1996.

Sue has a fantastic philosophy for herself and her players, and she provides a supportive environment both on and off the ice. Most of the players Sue coaches have careers, jobs, and a family life, leaving little time for sports. But having a supportive coach like Sue who understands the balance between playing at your best and meeting your life's responsibilities is a win/win situation for the athletes and the sport they love. "I don't coach athletes, I coach people. Bringing out the best in people brings out the best in athletes."

Sylvie Daigle started her illustrious speed skating career almost accidentally, with the intention of playing hockey. "I heard there was going to be hockey for girls at our local arena. I thought that was great so I went to sign up. There had been a mistake: the registration was for speed skating, not for hockey. I signed up anyway."

Sylvie was nine the first time she tried on a pair of speed skates in her hometown of Sherbrooke, Quebec. It didn't take long for her coach to realize she was a winner. By the time she was sixteen, she had won four gold medals at the 1979 Canada Winter Games. Since then Sylvie has participated in four Olympics, continuing her gold rush with another gold medal for speed skating at the 1992 Winter Olympics.

Hockey wasn't a key sport for girls in Sherbrooke, but Sylvie still managed to play her way onto the team that would represent Quebec at four National Championships. "I was twenty-four years old when I first played hockey for a real, competitive team. We went to the Nationals that year, and won. So, for anyone who thinks they're too old, it's never too late to start."

Sylvie says that most people don't realize what a big difference there is between speed skating and hockey. For instance, there are up to six inches of extra blade on a speed skate. "When I first started playing hockey again, after speed skating for several years, I had to use the boards to help me stand up. Although my speed skating experience gives me an advantage, I still need to practice with a stick and a puck."

Sylvie enjoys the team atmosphere of hockey and says the camaraderie gives her extra strength. "We're all in it together and this has such a strong effect; the spirit of struggling toward the same goal is something I've never felt before."

What's her secret to becoming a great hockey player? "Skating! Of course. I believe that what differentiates the average players and the best hockey players is their skating ability."

PRO FILE

SYLVIE DAIGLE

Skater with Style

Sylvie Daigle

CHAPTER 5

Goaltending

OWHA Archives

WHO IS THAT MYSTERIOUS GIRL BEHIND THE MASK?

There's something intriguing about a hockey goaltender. Maybe it's her mask? It hides her emotions. Even in the heat of the action, no one really knows what a goalie is thinking or feeling.

It takes a special kind of girl to be a goaltender — one who has quick reflexes, who likes to be challenged, and who doesn't mind a lot of responsibility.

In Chapter 4, I looked at the skills required to play forward and defense — skating, stickhandling, passing, and shooting. These are important skills for goaltenders to learn, in addition to special "netminding" concepts such as stance and angles.

A WORD ABOUT SAFETY

Goaltenders are the best-protected players on the ice. They wear thick layers of padding to cushion them from the bruising effects of the puck. They also have a circular "crease" — a specially marked area in front of the net indicating the zone that no offensive player is allowed to enter. In most cases, the goaltender should be the only player in the crease. Because of the crease, goaltenders generally encounter less body contact than other players, which means the risk of injury may also be lower.

15. Goaltender in stand-up stance

PLAYING GOAL

While an air of mystery surrounds the role of the goaltender, the truth is that this position requires as much athletic skill as any other. With practice, you can learn how to play goal and how to play it well.

Ian Young, one of North America's foremost goaltender coaches, has taught a lot of young goalies at his hockey school in Whitby, Ontario. He says many girls have natural abilities that help them to play goal. "Some girls are much more flexible and agile than boys. This is a definite advantage when it comes to playing goal. Many girls also have very good reflexes, and this allows them to react quickly to a shot."

When it comes to goalies, Ian knows what he's talking about. He's coached NHL stars such as Kelly Hrudey, Kirk McLean, Peter Sidorkiewicz, Damien Rhodes, and Jeff Hackett. Ian believes that skating is the key to becoming a successful goalie. "The best goalies today are the ones who are good skaters, who can move well from side to side, and who can drop to their knees and return to their feet quickly. My advice is this: work on your skating, and learn how to become involved in the play."

Stance

Standing Tall in the Net

"Stance" refers to the way a goaltender stands as she prepares to make a save. There are normally two positions: the "stand-up" stance and the "butterfly" stance. A stand-up goaltender keeps her legs fairly close together and doesn't drop down on the ice very often. A butterfly goaltender extends her legs further and goes down on the ice more often to make saves. In this position, her arms and legs tend to resemble the wings of a butterfly. (See Figures 15 and 16 for illustrations of these two types of goaltender stances.)

These days, the distinction between stand-up and butterfly goaltenders is not very noticeable. Because the game of hockey is so fast, most goalies use a combination stance, with their feet shoulder-width apart and their body fairly upright. This allows them to skate, to protect the low corners,

16. Goaltender in butterfly stance

and to go down quickly to their knees when necessary.

The following Stance Checklist runs through the most important points to remember. This checklist is easy to use. Have your coach or a parent or a friend evaluate your stance, circling the appropriate "yes" or "no" answers.

You should answer "yes" to every question, except numbers 6 and 7. The most important question is number 14. If you don't feel comfortable, you won't play well.

pro tip

EQUIPMENT CHECKLIST

1. Head
- ☐ mask with helmet
- ☐ throat protector
- ☐ neck protector

2. Arms, chest, and shoulders
- ☐ chest and arm protector
- ☐ trapper
- ☐ blocker
- ☐ sports bra

3. Lower body
- ☐ goalie pants
- ☐ pelvic protector
- ☐ goalie pads
- ☐ hockey socks
- ☐ garter

4. Feet
- ☐ goalie skates
- ☐ athletic socks

5. Other equipment
- ☐ goalie sticks
- ☐ tape
- ☐ equipment bag
- ☐ skate guards
- ☐ skate wipe

Stance Checklist

1.	Knees together?	yes	no
2.	Feet apart?	yes	no
3.	Knees slightly bent?	yes	no
4.	Shoulders in line with knees?	yes	no
5.	Head up?	yes	no
6.	Leaning too far forward?	yes	no
7.	Standing too straight?	yes	no
8.	Gloves at knee level?	yes	no
9.	Gloves just above the knee pads?	yes	no
10.	Trapper open all the time?	yes	no
11.	Hand over arch of stick?	yes	no
12.	Stick slightly in front of pads?	yes	no
13.	Stick blade flat on the ice?	yes	no
14.	Do you feel comfortable?	yes	no

(Adapted from *Behind the Mask,* by Ian Young and Chris Gudgeon. Used by permission of the authors.)

Angles

"Playing the angles." What does it mean? When a goaltender wants to make a save, she moves toward the puck shooter. For the best chance of making that save, she imagines a line running from the puck to the center of the goal line. This line should pass right between the middle of the goalie's feet. While it may take some time for this part of your game to improve, don't worry. It can take years for a goaltender to develop an inner sense for playing the angles.

Equipment: Protecting Young Goaltenders

The goaltender has a unique role on a hockey team — she is the only player whose specific task is to try to stop the puck from going into the net. Her equipment is very different from that of the other players, and this special equipment serves two purposes: it protects her from injury, and it allows her to cover more space in the net. The more space she covers, the more difficult it is for her opponents to score.

The goaltender is the best protected player on the ice. Her equipment usually costs more than anyone else's. A set of goalie leg pads, for example, could easily cost as much as the entire package of equipment for a forward or a defender. To combat these high costs, many minor leagues provide equipment, usually leg pads, gloves, and chest and arm protectors. Used equipment shops can also be very helpful.

If you're just starting out and you want your own equipment, there's nothing wrong with buying a used set of leg pads. It will save you the trouble of breaking in stiff new pads, and save your parents hundreds of dollars.

The pages that follow provide practical information about goaltender equipment. I'll tell you what each piece is for, how to use it, and offer a few tips on buying it.

HEAD

- Mask with helmet
- Throat protector
- Neck protector

Mask with Helmet

Goaltenders used to play without masks. Even up to the 1970s, some NHL goalies faced 100-mile-an-hour slap shots barefaced. Times have changed.

Now goaltenders must wear masks. There are two types of masks in common use today: the cage mask, made with thick metal wires and resembling a baseball catcher's mask, and the full, molded plastic or fiberglass mask. A goalie mask is usually sold with a helmet attachment, unless the mask is specially made-to-order.

Most minor league goalies use a cage mask. It has a couple of advantages: it keeps your head cooler, and also allows for the best view. But the molded mask is more durable, and absorbs the force of a shot better than the cage mask. That's why a lot of the goaltenders in the NHL, where the shots are much faster than in the minor leagues, wear a molded mask.

Some goalies, especially those at the minor level, use a cage-type mask with a plastic face guard. While this type of mask provides a good view of the ice, I don't recommend it because it fogs up easily and isn't as durable as other kinds of masks.

A lot of goaltenders are turning to a combination mask. It has a molded shell with a wire cage around the eyes and nose. This type of mask combines the best of both worlds: it stands up to the hardest of shots, but still keeps your head cool and offers a good look at the ice.

Used Masks

For health reasons, I don't recommend used masks. If you do buy one, make sure it has full head protection, especially at the back of the head. Sometimes, in a goal mouth scramble, a goalie's head may be smashed against the ice, so the back of the head must be protected.

Cost

Kids: $200 Cdn; $120 U.S.
Adult recreational: $250 Cdn; $150 U.S.
Adult competitive: $250 Cdn and up; $150 U.S. and up

Throat Protector and Neck Protector

A goaltender should always wear both a throat protector and a neck protector. A throat protector is a pad that looks something like a headband and fits comfortably around your neck. For more information, see the description in Chapter 3. The neck protector is a small piece of metal or plastic that hangs from the bottom of the mask. It not only protects against pucks and sticks, but also against the goalie's worst nightmare — a skate cut on the neck. Even the best neck protector is still relatively inexpensive (approximately $20 Cdn; $12 U.S.), so I strongly recommend that every goaltender wear one.

Cost

Neck Protector

    Kids: $20 Cdn; $12 U.S.

    Adults: $20 Cdn; $12 U.S.

Throat Protector

    Kids: $30 Cdn; $18 U.S.

    Adults: $30 Cdn; $18 U.S.

ARMS, CHEST, AND SHOULDERS

- Chest and arm protector
- Trapper
- Blocker
- Sports bra

Chest and Arm Protector

This used to be two separate pieces of equipment, but now it is normally one piece. You can cut corners when buying leg pads, pants, and even skates, but quality and fit in a chest and arm protector are more important than cost.

The chest protector is similar to the padded apron baseball catchers wear. It hangs loosely in front of the goalie and is worn underneath her sweater to protect her chest and stomach. This pad should also have flaps on each side to cover the kidneys, and should not fit too tightly. The loose fit allows it to cushion the force of the puck before the puck hits the body. However, this pad shouldn't be so big that it inhibits the goaltender's stance.

The arm protector consists of two quilted sleeves joined in the middle with a plastic plate. A good arm protector will provide protection for the shoulders — usually in the form of a plastic plate — and the arms to just above the wrists. Goalies are often given arm pads that are too short, which may leave the soft underside of the wrist exposed. The best arm pads cover the wrist and, like the chest pad, fit loosely to absorb shots. Also, look for arm pads that offer some protection to the inner elbows. Not all of them do.

Used Chest and Arm Protectors

The older style two-piece protectors, with separate chest and arm pieces, are fine. These tend to offer less protection for the upper chest — the breastbone and collarbone — and the back. You may want to add some extra padding in these areas. Never buy protective equipment like this if it's too small. A chest protector should fit loosely at the front, and arm pads should tuck at least one inch into your gloves.

Cost

Kids: $200 Cdn; $120 U.S.
Adults: $300 Cdn and up; $180 U.S. and up

Trapper and Blocker

A goaltender uses two kinds of gloves: the trapper, or catcher, and the blocker. Both gloves are available for either left-handed or right-handed players.

The trapper looks like a big baseball mitt. It has a large pad on the bottom that extends down to protect the underside of the goalie's wrist. This is the glove goaltenders use to catch the puck.

The blocker is a normal glove with a large rectangular pad attached to the top. Goalies wear this glove on their stick hand, and they use it to deflect shots away from the net. Some goaltenders bend the top pad of the blocker so that it resembles a big, flat banana. They do this because the bent pad acts to cushion a shot. Other goaltenders like to keep this pad as flat as possible, with only a slight bend. This allows them to cover more space with their blocker, and helps them to deflect the puck further away from the net.

Used Gloves

Used gloves can be a great bargain. But check for tears and for stitching that has come apart. If the damage is not too extensive, you can easily get the gloves repaired. Make sure that the trapper has a good solid pad to protect the wrist.

The glove on the blocker should be in good condition — this is the only protection your stick hand gets. Avoid blockers with big banana curves in the main pad: it's hard to flatten these out, and the big curve is not to most goalies' liking.

Costs (per pair)

Kids: $270 Cdn; $165 U.S. **Trapper** $140 Cdn; $85 U.S.
 Blocker $130 Cdn; $80 U.S.

Adults: $500 Cdn; $300 U.S. **Trapper** $250 Cdn; $150 U.S.
 Blocker $250 Cdn; $150 U.S.

Sports Bra

Cost

$30 Cdn; $18 U.S.

LOWER BODY

- Goalie pants
- Pelvic protector
- Goalie pads
- Hockey socks
- Garter

Goalie Pants

In the old days, all female hockey players, including goaltenders, wore skirts. This wasn't really a problem for them. The skirt helped stop the puck from slipping through the goalies' legs; some goalies even sewed lead weights into the hems of their skirts to give them an extra edge on low shots!

Nowadays, all hockey goaltenders wear pants. Goalie pants look like any other pair of hockey pants, but they have one important difference — lots of padding. Goalie pants are not required equipment, especially at younger levels, but they can help cut down on the number of bruises. Most brands made today don't require suspenders.

You can cheat a little. Goaltenders often stuff their pants with extra foam, plastic, or paper to give them added protection. One more tip: regardless of what kind of hockey pants you wear, make sure that they fit well under the top of your leg pads. Two inches of hockey pants under the leg pad will help ensure that your legs get the maximum amount of protection.

Used Goalie Pants

These can be a great bargain as long as they are clean and don't have any rips, tears, or missing padding. If you buy a used pair of pants, check to see if they require suspenders. Suspenders can be bought at most hockey supply stores.

Cost

Kids: $100 Cdn; $60 U.S.
Adults: $200 Cdn; $120 U.S.

Pelvic Protector

There are specially designed pelvic protectors for goaltenders that offer extra protection. Or, if you choose, you can use a regular "jill" with added padding. Some girls buy a goalie's jock, take out the hard plastic cup, and replace it with a more comfortable protective material.

Cost

Kids/Adults: $15 to $30 Cdn; $9 to $18 U.S.

Goalie Pads

Goalie pads protect a goaltender's legs. They also help her stop the puck because they take up so much space in the net. They are straightforward to use; straps are attached to hold them in place on your legs. Unlike other players' hockey socks, goalie socks go underneath, not over, your leg pads, and your hockey garter will make sure that your socks stay in place. Your skate fits through a horseshoe-shaped hole at the bottom of the pad, which allows the pad to reach

Barbara Stewart

almost to the ice. Even though the two pads look the same, there is a left one and a right one. Usually there is a vertical strip of padding, an inch or more thick, that runs along the outside edge of each pad.

When selecting leg pads, choose a pair that fits well above your knee; halfway up your thigh is ideal. A lot of goaltenders wear normal leg pads or good knee pads underneath their goalie pads. I recommend you do the same. Since goalie leg pads do not protect the sides of your knees very well, extra protection is a wise investment.

The biggest problem with leg pads is that they are quite heavy. A goaltender's pads can double in weight as they absorb water and perspiration. Regularly waxing your pads, or rubbing them with a special sealant, which cuts down on the amount of water they absorb, will help prevent moisture damage. Ask someone at a sports store to suggest a product. Equipment manufacturers are now coming out with lighter pads that absorb less water.

Used Goalie Pads

Once again, there is nothing wrong with used pads. I recommend that a growing or beginner goalie who must have her own pads consider used ones first. They are much cheaper, and are a better investment until you've stopped growing.

Look for a pair of pads with all the straps intact and a minimum of rips and tears. Since pads are made to be durable and flexible, they are very easy to repair.

Cost

Kids: $400 Cdn; $240 U.S.
Adults: $700 to $1,000 Cdn and up; $420 to $600 U.S. and up

FEET

- Goalie skates
- Athletic socks

Goalie Skates

Goalie skates look very much like regular skates, but there are two important differences. First, the goalie boot is thicker and has a plastic covering on the outside, which helps protect your foot. Second, the goalie blade is thicker and sturdier, and closer to the boot. A goaltender's skates take a lot of abuse, and have to be equal to the task. They also must be sharpened in a special way. While a forward's skates are sharpened to give her more speed, a goaltender's skates are sharpened to give her better balance and smoother lateral — or side-to-side — motion. For this reason, the bottom of a goalie's skate blade is flatter. Any good skate sharpener will know the proper way to fix up your goalie skates.

Used Goalie Skates

There's nothing wrong with used goalie skates. They seem to be a real bargain at most of the used equipment shops. One thing to check is the rivets on the bottom of the skate boot. These are the small metal tacks that connect the blade to the boot. There should be an even number of rivets, with at least four on either side of the blade. If a few rivets are missing, it doesn't mean the skates are no good, but you may have to pay a little extra to get them fixed. I think it's important for young goalies to learn to play on a good pair of proper goalie skates. You can scrimp on other equipment.

Cost
Kids: $170 Cdn; $110 U.S.
Adults: $200 Cdn and up; $120 U.S. and up

Athletic Socks

Cost

$5 Cdn; $3 U.S.

OTHER EQUIPMENT

- Goalie sticks
- Tape
- Equipment bag
- Skate guards
- Skate wipe

Goalie Sticks

A goalie stick looks like a wide hockey stick. The bottom half of the shaft, and the entire blade, is flat and wide. It is designed to block shots.

Quite often you hear people talk about the "lie" of a stick. The lie is the angle between the shaft and the blade of your stick. The shorter the goaltender, the lower number lie she will use. You can find the number of the lie on the back of the stick, near the top. Normally, the lie starts at twelve and goes up to fifteen. The best way to tell if your stick has the proper lie is to assume your stance with skates on. If the bottom of your stick lies flat on the ice, then you have the right lie.

One more tip: tape. Use tape, and lots of it, especially at the end of the handle. Smart goaltenders like to put a big roll of tape at the top of their stick. This lifts the stick handle off the ice, and makes it easier to pick up the stick if you drop it.

Used Goalie Sticks

If you find a stick with minimal cracks and chips, buy it. To check to see if there are any hidden cracks in the stick, bang it gently on the floor. If you hear a solid "thud," the stick is okay. If you hear a vibrating noise, the stick is cracked.

Cost

Kids: $45 Cdn; $25 U.S.

Adults: $60 Cdn and up; $35 U.S. and up

Equipment Bag

Cost

Kids: $50 Cdn; $30 U.S.

Adults: $80 Cdn; $50 U.S.

Skate Guards

Cost

Kids/Adults: $8 Cdn; $5 U.S.

On September 11, 1992, Manon Rhéaume made hockey history. She attended the Tampa Bay Lightning training camp — the first woman ever to try out for an NHL team. A publicity stunt? "No way!" said the Lightning management.

According to Manon, everyone was skeptical, but once they saw how she played, they quickly changed their tune. "The first time I tried out for the team, I had a shutout. I hadn't even practiced with them yet, but when I played during the second period, I didn't allow any goals. Everyone began to take me more seriously and I gained more respect because I stood my ground against the bigger players."

Manon so impressed everyone at her tryouts that she was signed on as a free agent by Tampa Bay before she was sent down to the minors. She spent several weeks practicing with the Lightning's farm team, the Atlanta Knights, to gain more experience. The Knights, an International Hockey League team, provided Manon with her first start in April 1993 against Cincinnati.

Manon had made history earlier by becoming the first woman to appear in a Major Junior hockey game. On November 26, 1991, Manon skated out to the Trois-Rivières Draveurs' net midway through a game against the Granby Bisons, with the score tied at 5–5. Manon gave up three goals and was tagged with the loss in a 10–6 Granby win. For seventeen minutes and thirteen shots, Manon got her start playing in the major leagues. "I could have played better, but I was very nervous. My playing has improved tremendously since then," Manon says confidently. Manon's confidence made her a celebrity. She presented the Vezina Trophy at the NHL's 1991 annual awards gala.

Manon had once considered making her name in alpine skiing, and eventually had to choose between that sport and hockey. It's not hard to see that her

MANON RHÉAUME

Rhéaume at the Top

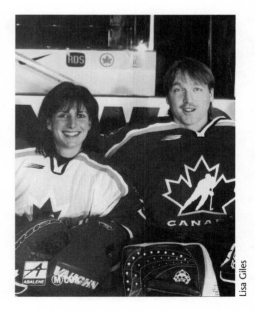

Manon Rhéaume and Patrick Roy.

Lisa Giles

decision has paid off. "I've always concentrated on my job as goaltender, not on making it into the NHL. I didn't want to put that kind of pressure on myself."

Manon's talent propelled her into the international limelight. She helped lead Canada to a gold medal in the Women's World Championships in April 1992, and was named to the All-Star team.

Manon says that, in terms of skill, there's not much difference between top-notch female and male players, but that the two games are played in somewhat different ways. "The men are stronger, more physical, and will try to intimidate me by rushing the net. And the shots are harder. But women players tend to be craftier, and use their stickhandling and skating skills more." Manon explains how she made her style of goaltending match each style of play. "When I'm playing with women, I have to adjust my timing because the shots on goal are slower, but women also tend to keep the puck in play much longer. The tryouts for the NHL and the Women's National Team were two very different experiences, and I wouldn't trade either for anything."

Manon says the secret to her success as a goaltender is that she moves well on her feet, and she's aggressive in the play. "I like to challenge shooters; you have to play well these days, so I'll come out of my net if I have to. But I can also butterfly quite well to cover all my angles. I also work very hard on my skating, a goalie has to be able to move quickly. The art of goaltending is really the art of concentrating and being in position."

Despite all the attention she's received from hockey, Manon says that her dream is to work in television. "Hockey is something that I enjoy doing. I'll always play hockey, but I've wanted to work in television since I was a young girl. In the future, I'm going to devote the same energy to my career as I devoted, in the past, to hockey."

Manon's career in television will have to take a back seat for a while, since her interest in hockey has continued to keep her in the news. To date, she has played hockey as long as some professional NHL players, for more than nineteen years. After making it *safe* for women to play hockey, Manon is still tending goal for the big boys. She plays for the Reno Renegades of the West Coast Hockey League, and still had time to make the tryouts for the 1998 Olympic Team.

The highlights of Manon's hockey life to date include being a goalkeeper for the gold medal team during the 1994 World Championships held in Lake Placid, New York, where she was named to the All-Star team (with a 1.72 goals-against average in four games). She was a member of the gold medal team at the 1996 Pacific Rim Championships, held in Richmond, B.C. In 1996 and 1997 she was a goalkeeper at the Three Nations Cup, in Ottawa and Lake Placid, where Team Canada won gold and silver, respectively. Manon was named to the 1998 Olympic Team on December 9, 1997, and proudly brought home a silver medal from the Olympic Games in Nagano, Japan.

PRO FILE

SARAH COUCH

Bowmanville Backstop

Sarah Couch started playing hockey when she was only five years old. She borrowed some equipment and her dad signed her up. The other players on Sarah's first team were boys. Until 1994, she played for a boys' team, the Bowmanville Eagles, an OHA Junior C team. "The other players treated me the same as anyone else," she says. "The only people it ever seemed to bother were the parents."

Sarah decided to become a goalie in the same way most people do — by accident. The team didn't have a regular goalie, so she had to take her turn in the net. She was hooked. "I enjoyed keeping the players from scoring; that was the best part."

Goalie equipment is not cheap, so Sarah would get a summer job when she was younger, and her parents would help out with the rest of the costs. "If you look around, you can always find good deals on equipment. Of course, I have to try on a lot of equipment to find pieces that fit just right. I'm pretty fussy when I choose a chest protector; I want one that's comfortable, but still has lots of padding."

Sarah has never been afraid of getting hurt. She suffers the normal things, like muscle pulls, but she doesn't worry too much about injuries because "there's no sense in playing if you're afraid all the time."

Most of Sarah's friends are very supportive, and often come out to watch her play. Her on-ice dramatics have inspired some of her girlfriends to sign up. "They're always asking, 'How can I play?' They sign up for girls' hockey, which is lots of fun, and they love it."

Sarah moved to women's hockey in 1994 when she began to play for the Toronto Aeros, where she tended goal for two years. She then played for the Newtonbrook Panthers, and now plays for the Oshawa Chinooks. Sarah made a lot of friends while goaltending for these women's teams, and saw several of her teammates make the Olympic Team. She still skates with a few men's teams whenever she can, just to stay on top of her game, but her goal is to make the 2002 Olympic Games in Salt Lake City, Utah, and to bring home a gold medal for backstopping her team to glory.

PRO FILE

DANIELLE DUBÉ

West Coast Winner

Andrew Glowinkowski

Danielle Dubé is a female first in British Columbia. She followed in Manon Rhéaume's footsteps to become the first female to play in the British Columbia Junior Hockey League. Danielle, who hails from Vancouver, was netminder for the Grandview Midget AA team in the Pacific Coast Amateur Hockey Association, where she was the only female goaltender in that league.

Danielle has an extensive list of accomplishments, including a silver medal for backstopping the British Columbia team in the 1991 Canada Winter Games. She helped Grandview to a 29–9–3 record in the 1992–1993 season, and was constantly credited with spectacular saves in local papers reporting her wins.

Danielle's interest in hockey was sparked when she watched her father play in his firefighters' league. The next year, when she was four, she signed up to play hockey. "Even though there were only male teams, I joined anyway. I took some power skating classes, and played out for the first two years. I didn't start in goal until I was six. A goalie coach came in and said I was a good technical skater, and asked if I'd like to try goaltending. I tried it and thought it was great."

For Danielle, it's good to know that her teammates feel confident and inspired when she's in net. "I'm steady and consistent and I have good concentration. I'm known as a stand-up goalie: I have no fear of challenging the shooters."

Danielle tried out for the National team at the age of fifteen. She didn't make it then, but was selected to the National Team to play at the U.S. Olympic Festival in San Antonio, Texas, in 1993, where her team won a silver medal. "I'm just like any young player who has dreams of playing in the NHL. I'd love to have the chance, and I know I can go that far. I want to play hockey for as long as I can."

Danielle certainly has a promising hockey career ahead of her. She has played for over thirteen years in the Grandview Minor Hockey Association in Vancouver, where her Junior B team, the Grandview Steelers, were Provincial Champions in the 1993–1994 season. She has also played for the Abbotsford Pilots (Junior B) and the Penticton Panthers, a Junior A team. She made her mark in the Western Professional Hockey League, playing goalie for the Central Texas Stampede, in their 1996–1997 season. And her National Team involvement has been very impressive to date. Besides being a Team Canada member at the U.S. Olympic Festival in San Antonio, she was also a gold medal team member in the 1995 and 1996 Pacific Rim Championships. Danielle was a member of the gold medal team during the 1996 Three Nations Cup in Ottawa. She also played in the 1997 World Championships in Kitchener, Ontario, where she took home another gold medal.

Unfortunately, Danielle was cut from the 1998 Olympic team going to Nagano, but she took it in stride.

"I'm young, I figure I have at least two more Olympics I can compete in, and it was a tough spot to fill. I was up against more experienced team members like Manon Rhéaume and Lesley Reddon."

There's still Salt Lake City in 2002, Danielle.

CHAPTER 6

Team Works

"BEATRICE AEROS"
1998 TEAM ONTARIO

The 1998 Beatrice Aeros.

Maria Quinto

WOMEN'S HOCKEY PROGRAMS FROM COAST TO COAST

So you've made up your mind that you want to play hockey. Or maybe you're already on a team and you want to move to a higher level of play. The question is: How do you find a team that's best suited to your needs?

The CHA and USA Hockey

No matter where you live in North America, you can get help from one of two national hockey organizations. In Canada, that organization is the Canadian Hockey Association (CHA). In the United States, USA Hockey (USAH) will be glad to help. CHA's main office is in Ottawa; you can reach it by calling (613) 748–5613. USAH is based in Colorado Springs, Colorado; their telephone number is (719) 599–5500. You can also reach both of these organizations on the Internet. The CHA's Web address is www.canadianhockey.ca. USAH's address is www.usahockey.com.

Both organizations have special departments that oversee women's hockey programs. They can tell you how to find a team, or how to organize your own women's league. They are also a great source of books, pamphlets, videos, and other resource material.

Both CHA and USAH have regional branches. For more information, see the list of addresses at the back of this book. The branch offices are your best bet for getting detailed information about hockey programs in your area.

Ages and Stages

In Canada, hockey players progress through a series of leagues aimed at specific age groups. CHA leagues are *usually* arranged in these categories.

Tykes	6 and under
Novice	9 and under
Atom	11 and under
PeeWee	13 and under
Bantam	15 and under
Midget	17 and under
Minor	19 and under
Junior	20 and under
Senior	open age

The CHA also offers a special initiation program designed to make children's first contact with hockey a safe and positive experience, while introducing beginners to the game's basic skills.

Since women's hockey programs strive to be player-centered, age categories do not always apply. When necessary, different age groups and skill levels are often combined to form teams. As more and more women register for hockey, eventually there will be complete teams in all age divisions. For now, women's hockey programs tend to have a somewhat informal structure; anyone can join a team, at any age or skill level.

Within each age group there are also two levels of teams: house and rep. House teams play in a league made up of teams based in one club or arena. Rep teams — that's short for "representative" — are usually made up of the club's top players in an age group, or of players who are interested in more competitive play. Rep teams play in a league made up of teams from different clubs.

Players in their late teens also have the option of playing for their high school hockey team, and when they are finished high school, they can play for their university or college. In the university system, there are usually three levels of play: recreational leagues; intramural or house leagues; and varsity teams, which represent the school in games against other rep teams. When registering for college or university, ask the athletic department about women's hockey programs. They probably have one that suits you. For more information, check the listings at the back of this book.

In the United States there are five classifications of women's hockey:

1. *Initiation:* The first level of hockey that offers young girls the opportunity to learn to skate in a fun environment. The fundamental skills of the game are taught in a noncompetitive atmosphere.

2. *Recreation:* Recreation or house league teams tend to be the backbone of all USAH programs. Recreational hockey is usually played at a local rink, and fun, skill, and friendship are stressed as part of the game. As in Canada, players develop through a system of age-related leagues:

   PeeWee   15 and under
   Midget   19 and under
   Senior   20 and over

3. *Select:* Select teams are for those who want to play in a more competitive arena. Affiliates may include local All-Star teams, travel teams, and local and regional development camps. A player on a select team can increase her skill level, learn team concepts, and compete for local, regional, state, and USAH National Championships. Leagues progress the same as in recreational hockey.

4. *High School and Prep School:* High schools and prep schools offer both club and varsity hockey. Various levels of competition are designed for the serious female athlete.

5. *Collegiate:* As in high school and prep school hockey, there are two levels of collegiate hockey: club and varsity. Club teams play in in-house leagues and against club teams from other colleges. Varsity teams represent their school at the intercollegiate level — the highest level of women's hockey in the U.S. According to USAH, there are more than fifty women's college varsity and college club teams across the country. With the support of the National Collegiate Athletic Association, the Eastern College Athletic Conference (ECAC) now sponsors two leagues for women — the ECAC Women's Hockey League, a Division I league comprising strictly varsity-level teams, and the ECAC Women's Hockey Alliance, a Division III league comprising both varsity and club teams. More and more colleges and universities are upgrading their women's hockey programs to varsity status.

William Bellsey

Getting ready to play in the first ever Northwest Territorials, 1991.

STARTING YOUR OWN ASSOCIATION

A Guide for Players and Their Parents

So, you want to play hockey but there is no girls' league in your hometown. You can register in a boys' league, but remember, body checking may be permitted, and it may not be much fun if you're the only girl on the team. The boys have probably been playing hockey for years and may be very competitive, with a more aggressive style of play. This may not be what you are looking for.

What should you do now? Why not create your own association? Here are some basic guidelines to help you set up and develop an association for girls' hockey. They are based on the Ontario Women's Hockey Association's (OWHA) development program.

Step 1: Contact

Your first step is to contact your provincial or state hockey association and ask for help in organizing an "initiative meeting," a gathering of everyone interested in starting a women's hockey program. You should also contact your local recreation department to advise them of your plans.

Your local hockey association should be able to provide you with plenty of resource material — brochures, pamphlets, promotional videos, and general information about the rules and guidelines of hockey in your area — which you can distribute at your meeting.

Step 2: Make a Date

Next you must decide on a date and time for the meeting. Book a hall or a room, or even a public meeting place with lots of space. Give yourself plenty of time to round up prospective players, coaches and interested people. Book the room well in advance, say, three to five months.

Step 3: Publicity

Ask four or five of your friends to help you publicize the meeting. You want it to be successful, so it's important that everyone know about it.

Prepare posters to be placed all over town. Put the date, time, and place in big bold letters, stating that everyone — players, coaches, referees, and parents — is welcome to get involved in women's hockey. Put posters up in ice rinks, arenas, sports stores, community centers, libraries, store windows, malls, and in local restaurants where kids hang out.

You can also send a letter indicating what you are doing, as well as flyers and brochures, to the principals of schools located in your area. Prepare enough packages for all the elementary and secondary schools in the local board of education. Remember to include the separate and private schools as well.

And don't forget to use the media. Send a press release and a copy of your poster to all the newspapers, radio stations, and TV stations in your area. Local media often run community service programs that may provide advertising free of charge, so be persistent.

Finally, don't forget to tell everyone you know about the meeting: word of mouth is great advertising.

Step 4: The Meeting

Prepare the meeting room with a few tables to display material, and if you can find a coffee machine and some cookies, great! Put a clipboard, with a pen and paper attached, near the door so that you can get the name and address of everyone who comes to the meeting.

Who should talk at the meeting? How about some local hockey players? The director of your regional hockey association probably will be happy to help.

Remember: this meeting is for information sharing, and will enable you to determine the amount of local interest. It is a good time to allay fears or questions about girls playing hockey. The message you want to get across is that it's healthy, fun, and safe for girls to play hockey.

At the end of the meeting, form a committee of three to four people. The purpose of this committee is to actively pursue the formal establishment of a women's hockey program in your area.

Step 5: Follow Up

After the first meeting, you'll need to take further steps to ensure that your organization will be sufficiently recognized. To begin with, meet with your local recreation department or municipality. Bring your girls' hockey organization plans along. Ask that these local organizations officially recognize your committee.

Put in a request for ice time at one of your local rinks. Most often, you will have to apply through the municipality, or ask your local minor league hockey association. The amount of ice time you require will be based on the number of teams you have planned. Since you have an official organization, you are entitled to a special ice rental rate at most arenas.

For information on available funding through government programs, contact your regional tourism or recreation office in Canada, or USA Hockey in the U.S.

Step 6: Recruitment

Once you have an organization, how do you go about getting players? The key is publicity. First, print up a brochure that states your association's objectives.

List the committee members' names, addresses, and phone numbers. Provide information on how to register.

Distribute these brochures to a wide range of groups: schools, churches, community groups, other girls' sports teams (such as softball, soccer, basketball), and boys' minor hockey associations (remember that a lot of these guys have sisters who might be interested in hockey).

Another way to advertise is to set up information booths at local malls, fairs, and bazaars. And don't forget to use local media: a classified ad is often a good, inexpensive way to recruit players.

THE CANADIAN HOCKEY HALL OF FAME

The Hockey Hall of Fame in Toronto made hockey history. It cost over $24 million to build in 1992, and is a spectacular look at the history of Canada's national game. The various exhibits offer an inspiring glimpse at both professional and amateur hockey over the past one hundred years. Special features include a photo library, hockey archives, large theater screens, and play-by-play broadcast booths. The building is a showcase for past and present players, teams, and leagues, and is designed to replicate historical hockey settings.

The best part? Why, the women's hockey section, of course! There are profiles of women's teams, and of individual personalities and players, through displays, artifacts, and multimedia presentations.

The Centre of Excellence, a satellite operation of Hockey Canada's Centre of Excellence based in Calgary, is located in the Hockey Hall of Fame and features resource material as well as coaching, officiating, training, and instructional films. For further information on the Hockey Hall of Fame or the Centre of Excellence, contact:

Hockey Hall of Fame, BCE Place
30 Yonge Street
Toronto, ON M5E 1X8
(416) 360-7765
www.hhof.com

Hockey Hall of Fame admission prices: adults $10.00, children (13 and under) $5.50, and seniors $5.50.

THE U.S. HOCKEY HALL OF FAME

The U.S. Hockey Hall of Fame is located in Eveleth, Minnesota, sixty miles north of Duluth. This nonprofit organization dedicated to the sport of hockey opened in 1973 and has lots of interesting exhibits, including a 1950s Zamboni, films and a theater, profiles of Hall of Fame inductees, Olympic displays, and other hockey history. The price is right; at $2.50 U.S. for adults and $1.50 U.S. for children, you can't go wrong. Although the women's hockey section is small, since they've just started putting it together, it's still worth the trip to Eveleth. For more information, contact:

United States Hockey Hall of Fame
801 Hat Trick Avenue
P.O. Box 567
Eveleth, MN 55734
(218) 744-5167
Gift Shop: 1-800-443-7825 or 1-800-HHF-PUCK
www.ushockeyhall.com

WOMEN'S PROFESSIONAL HOCKEY LEAGUE

The prospect of a professional hockey league for women looms large on the horizon. A pre-season camp is set to open on October 18, 1998, and there are five finalists in the franchise site selection: the Tri-Town Arena in Hookset, New Hampshire; the New England Sports Center in Marlboro, Massachusetts; the Tully Forum in Billerica, Massachusetts; the Sportplexe Pierrefonds, in Pierrefonds, Quebec; and Bridgeport Waterfront in Bridgeport, Connecticut. There may also be a partnership in the Toronto, Ontario, area.

PRO FILE

ANDRIA HUNTER

Hockey Grrrl

Andria Hunter

Andria Hunter is well known around the world. She's the one responsible for women's hockey — on the Internet that is! Andria has links to more than five hundred different women's hockey sites from her Web page at www.whockey.com.

It started when Andria was attending the University of Toronto; she decided to make herself a home page as a challenge. As she was surfing the Web for women's hockey links, she was astonished to discover that none could be found. So Andria took it upon herself to create a centralized index for women's hockey information.

Since their creation in the fall of 1994, the women's hockey web pages have really taken off. There is currently information on women's hockey in twenty-three different countries, university hockey results, and results from international competitions. And for anyone who wants to find out more about women's hockey — in Canada, the U.S., internationally, or even locally — she has it all. Some of the statistics on her women's hockey site include:

- over seven hundred pages and numerous graphic files
- users from seventy-nine different countries
- highest volume of visitors are from the U.S.A., Canada, and Europe
- on average, receives about six thousand hits or clicks every day!

Andria loves all sports, but is especially fond of hockey. She started her hockey career in 1976, when she signed on to play with a boys' minor hockey team in Peterborough, but switched to a girls' team the following year. "I started skating when I was four, on the pond on our farm just east of Peterborough, Ontario. While I was in my third year of figure skating, I asked my mom if I could play hockey the next year. My parents agreed, and I started playing on a boys' house league team when I was eight years old."

Hockey is popular in Peterborough, so Andria had no trouble finding a girls' team to play on. She also played for her high school, and they won the hockey championships in four out of the five seasons she was there. She attended the University of New Hampshire (UNH) on a full hockey scholarship, where she received the Rookie of the Year Award in 1987, the Wildcat Winners Club Scholar-Athlete Award in 1989, and the Alumni Association Student-Athlete Award in 1990. Andria was the leading scorer for UNH for three years, and earned over 170 points. Andria went to Switzerland for the 1992–1993 season and played for the DHC Langenthal hockey team of the Swiss Women's A League, where she quickly became one of the high scorers.

Andria continued her education at the University of Toronto. While finishing her master's degree in computer science, she played for the Varsity Blues. They won the Ontario Women's Interuniversity Athletic Association (OWIAA) championship four out of the five years that she was on the team (1990–1996).

Andria was selected to the gold medal-winning Team Canada in 1992 and 1994, playing at the Women's World Championships, held in Tampere, Finland, and Lake Placid, New York. She became one of the highest scorers, with five goals and four assists in five games during the 1992 series.

She also plays roller hockey during the summer, and won a gold medal with her team, the Toronto Tornado, at the 1996 North American Roller Hockey Championship in Chicago. "I started playing a little pickup in-line hockey with some guys in Toronto, and then in 1995 Sandy Nimmo put together the Toronto Tornado team that competed at the 1995 NARHC."

Since then, Andria has earned two more gold medals at the 1997 USA Hockey Inline Cup and the Canadian Hockey Inline Nationals. She was chosen 1997

Inline Hockey News Amateur female athlete of the year, having been the top scorer at all five tournaments, scoring a total of ninety-two points (forty-nine goals, forty-three assists) in twenty-six tournament games.

"I really enjoy playing in-line hockey! For me, the differences provide new challenges. It was like a breath of fresh air to try a new sport that is so similar to a sport that I love so much. I also like the fact that I can lace on my in-line skates and just go to an outdoor arena in Toronto any time I like."

In June 1993, Nancy Scholz was going for the gold. "I'm going to make the Canadian National Team tryouts, and then go to the Olympics to win a gold medal."

Those were high hopes for a young girl, but then again, Nancy wasn't just any young girl. She started playing house hockey when she was three. She wore her brother's equipment around the house and pretended to play. She was a pro by the time she got her first pair of hockey skates. Well, almost. "I was used to figure skates, so when I first tried to skate in hockey skates I fell over a lot."

Nancy grew up in a small community three hundred miles north of Whitehorse, Yukon, and finding a girls' hockey team was tough. In fact, even finding a boys' team was a challenge. "I wanted to play hockey, so the boys' team said okay — they needed the bodies on the ice. At the first practice, some of the guys were surprised to see me, and some were even embarrassed."

In 1990, the Scholz family moved to Whitehorse, and Nancy was disappointed to learn that there wasn't a girls' hockey league there either. Nancy had wanted to continue playing hockey, and eventually compete for a spot on the National Team, but that seemed almost impossible now. Without a registered league, players weren't eligible to compete in the National Team tryouts.

Nancy's mother, Mary, knew how much hockey meant to her daughter. So Mary and several other interested parents decided to form a girls' league. "It was a tough sell, but now we have a girls' team," explains Mary. "It was difficult at first and sometimes still is." She encountered some resistance when she started encouraging girls to join their local minor hockey association. Other parents became upset when they thought the girls were taking ice time away from the boys. "There are still some parents who think hockey belongs to their sons, but that attitude is wrong. Hockey is a game for everyone to enjoy."

Mary Scholz

Nancy played on the boys' team and in the girls' league her mother helped set up. Juggling two teams and a high school curriculum was hard work, so she opted for the most regular hours and played with the women's team. "It's difficult to find the time for everything, but I manage. And I always finish my homework," said Nancy at the time.

In fact, Nancy finished her homework so well she is currently studying kinesiology at the University of Calgary. Between her studies and playing defense for the University of Calgary Dino varsity women's team, she finds time to practice with her other team, the Olympic Oval Extreme, an AAA team that won gold at the Nationals in March 1998.

Nancy has followed through on her desire to play hockey, and has won several medals over the past few years. These include a bronze at the 1993 Western Canadian Shield Championships (WCSC) and two golds in 1994, one at the Arctic Winter Games held in Slave Lake, Alberta, and the other at the WCSC in Calgary, Alberta. Nancy also won a silver medal for her participation in the 1995 WCSC in Fort St. John, B.C. And 1996 saw both a silver and a gold win at the Arctic Winter Games in Eagle River, Alaska, and the WCSC in Winnipeg, Manitoba, respectively.

For now, Nancy is pleased with the path her hockey career has taken. "After leaving Whitehorse, I found that there were so many more people interested in women's hockey, and because of the level of play and the number of serious players, I've adjusted my goals so that they are realistic and attainable. I'm perfectly happy to keep playing for my varsity team, and hope to someday win a gold medal at Nationals with my AAA team."

CHAPTER 7

Coaching Corner

Karen Kay, head coach, 1994 U.S. National team.

Lynn Olson

A COACH FOR ALL SEASONS

Maybe you'd like to be involved in women's hockey but have finished your playing days, or you play and want to coach. Coaching is a great way for parents, friends, and former players to participate. At all levels of the game, positive and motivated coaches are in demand.

At the younger levels, where the players are twelve and under, a parent is often ideal. To become a good coach, you'll need special training and commitment. But the best coaches aren't necessarily the ones looking to make a professional career in coaching; they are often those who do it simply because they want to get involved, love the sport, or have children who play.

THE RIGHT STUFF

What makes a good coach? Every good coach needs these three qualities:

1. *Leadership.* Is she a good leader and a good role model? Is she the type of person you would like to have teach your children? It's important that coaches be able to teach not just hockey skills, but valuable individual life skills, team skills, and social interaction among players.
2. *Organizational ability.* Does the coach plan ahead to get the most out of the season? Is she prepared to meet the needs of her players? Does she have an appropriate practice plan?

3. *Personality*. Is the coach the type of person you want your child to be associated with? It is important to have trust in the coach. In some cases, a coach will spend more time with a child than a parent does.

NATIONAL COACHING CERTIFICATION PROGRAM

All coaches should have a certain level of training. Coaches involved with competitive teams need more training than others. In Canada, the National Coaching Certification Program (NCCP) is an educational program delivered by the Canadian Hockey Association that provides the training, structure, and necessary skills to become an effective coach.

There are three basic components within the NCCP: technical, theory, and practical. The technical teaches the skills, tactics, and systems of the sport, as well as information on rules of play and equipment. The theory provides generic principles of coaching such as planning, growth and development, safety, and skill analysis. And the practical component involves the application of the technical and theoretical in both on-ice and off-ice situations.

The NCCP offers four progressive stages of certification.

1. *Coach Level:* An entry level for beginner coaches, or for those who have a minimal amount of experience. The focus is on the role of the coach, and how to combine fun with learning, and team participation with self-

confidence. Coach level emphasizes basic skills and the importance of having players develop confidence, self-esteem, and a love for the game.

2. *Intermediate Level:* This level takes a deeper look at the coaching process and examines how team play concepts and individual tactics can be combined in competitive hockey. At this level, the coach must demonstrate leadership, deal with injuries, and communicate with parents, referees, support staff, and hockey administrators.

3. *Advanced Level 1:* Designed for coaches who want to develop a structured and disciplined approach to hockey. Such coaches should already have several years of experience at the competitive level. Among other topics, this course covers nutrition, stress management, player motivation, skills analysis, and the interpretation of statistics.

4. *Advanced Level II:* Coaches who take this course are prepared for leadership roles in national and international hockey. The course is based on a twelve task credit system. Coaches receive credits after successfully completing each task. The final level of certification ensures that all coaches have completed the corresponding group work, take-home assignments, and field evaluations, which are directly linked to the Canadian Hockey Association's Level 4 program designed for high performance coaching.

For more information about the NCCP, contact your nearest Canadian Hockey Association branch office.

USA HOCKEY'S COACHING ACHIEVEMENT PROGRAM

USA Hockey has established a dual coaching education system consisting of a volunteer track and a career track. Since 1996, all USA Hockey coaches, assistants, and instructors are expected to meet certain standardized requirements. Here is a brief description of the volunteer track guidelines:

1. *Course Level:* A course or initiation program instructor is allowed to coach Mites travel teams, Learn to Skate, Atoms, Mighty Mites, and the initiation program.
2. *Associate Level:* This level allows instructors to coach Squirt travel and house teams, and other house teams in PeeWee, Bantam, and Midget. The clinic is a one-day training session that deals with all aspects of coaching, including, but not restricted to, planning, techniques, concepts, drills, communication, and training, as well as other required coaching ethics and standards.
3. *Intermediate Level:* An intermediate level coach can coach PeeWee, Bantam, and Junior C travel teams, and house teams in Bantam and Midget.
4. *Advanced Level:* The advanced level permits instructors to coach a high caliber of youth hockey, including Midget, high school (club varsity), prep school (all divisions), and Junior A and B.

The career track includes the advanced level, master level, elite level, and high performance level. More information on this coaching program can be obtained by contacting USA Hockey.

"Women's hockey is gradually changing for the better; it won't be as tough for the next generation as it was for me. Am I a trailblazer? Well, maybe!"

Karen Kay *is* a trailblazer. She has been playing hockey since she was nine years old, having fallen in love with the game in the days when Bobby Orr ruled the ice. Growing up in Marlboro, Massachusetts, she was the only skater in her family and played on one of the first female leagues.

Karen attended Providence College on a hockey scholarship. A serious shoulder injury during a hockey game caused her to be sidelined during her senior year. But she stayed on with the team and became the student assistant coach. "During college, I coached at the high school level. It was a high caliber of youth hockey; we played a college schedule, against college teams, winning most of the time, so I was happy. After I graduated, I found myself turning down several opportunities to coach at the college level simply because the positions were part-time."

Karen's coaching career developed gradually. She started out with PeeWee players, then moved up to the Midget level, leading her team to two U.S. National Championships. When the job of coaching at the University of New Hampshire (UNH) opened up, Karen jumped at the chance. "I had coached most of the players. In fact, there were only a few players who I hadn't coached at some point in their hockey careers. It was a nice reunion for me."

Karen was the first woman to be selected as head coach for the 1994 U.S. National Team. That announcement came at a very timely moment for women's hockey — on the eve of its being granted Olympic status.

In 1993, Karen led Team USA to wins over Team Canada at the first-ever North American Challenge and the U.S. Olympic Festival in San Antonio, Texas. Karen

Eileen Raleigh, UNH Instructional Services

was behind the bench when Team USA captured the silver medal at the 1994 World Championships in Lake Placid, New York. She was subsequently named the recipient of USA Hockey's prestigious Bob Johnson Medallion for her contribution to international hockey. Karen also coached the American team to a silver medal finish in the 1995 Pacific Rim Championships held in San Jose, California.

Karen went back to UNH, and is now entering her sixth year behind the bench of one of the most successful women's collegiate hockey programs in the country. USA Hockey selected Karen as one of three head coaches for the 1997 Women's National Festival in Lake Placid, New York, which served as the evaluation camp for the selection of the 1997 U.S. National Team.

Karen hopes her determination and perseverance will open doors for other women who want to pursue the same goals. And hopefully they won't have to fight as hard as she did. For Karen, it's been a steady battle, with a rewarding goal for which she's worked long and hard. Thanks to her trailblazing tactics, more females will be qualified to coach higher levels of hockey.

SHANNON MILLER

Excel Hockey Coach

Shannon Miller polices the ice when she coaches her team, and when she's off ice, she's a police officer in Calgary, Alberta. "I believe that coaches have an incredible impact on athletes. We really can make a difference, and it's a great way to get involved in something that encourages positive growth in young people."

Shannon grew up in Melfort, Saskatchewan, and played with a girls' team that stayed together throughout high school and university. They called themselves the Saskies and won several Provincial Championships, and attended many National Championships.

Shannon played with the Saskies until 1986, while finishing her degree at the University of Saskatchewan. She then moved to Calgary where she started coaching after helping to develop the first-ever girls' minor hockey team in 1989. The Calgary Cougars became the first girls' team to play in a boys' hockey league. Shannon also instructed at the Alberta Identification Camp held for the Canada Winter Games, and subsequently was hired on as a member of the coaching staff. Alberta won the gold medal at the 1991 Canada Winter Games in Prince Edward Island, the first year that women's hockey was included in the Games. In June 1991, Shannon was named assistant coach to Team Canada. Shannon was also head coach for Team Alberta at the first-ever Junior National Championships in 1993, which were held in Montreal for girls under eighteen years of age. "The high caliber of the young players left me speechless. I knew there was talent out there, but I didn't realize there was so much; these players are our future National Team members."

Shannon fulfills the requirements necessary to be an influential coach; she is an inspirational leader and a good communicator with a positive outlook and

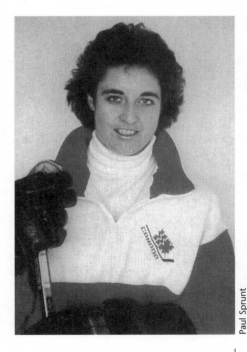

Paul Sprunt

133

an exceptional knowledge of the game of hockey. She has completed the advanced coach level, and has continued to improve her coaching skills. "Most coaches are great volunteers and love the game. I feel it's important to have a working knowledge of the technical and strategic aspects of the game, especially if you are coaching at a high level of competition."

When the Canadian National Team won the gold medal at the World Championships in 1992, Shannon's experience as assistant coach was exactly what she had expected. "We succeeded in putting together a winning team by developing the players both on and off the ice. We created a positive, fun team environment, which produced a team that was totally committed to winning. It was a great experience."

As a matter of fact, the coaching staff built the players up so much they were like steamrollers in the final game of the World Championships. The Canadians were tight, together, and tough — they felt untouchable. Shannon believes the National Team has a reputation to uphold. After all, hockey is Canada's game!

Shannon's impressive career made her the logical choice as head coach for Canada's Olympic Team. She was the first-ever full-time salaried head coach of Canada's women's team and the only full-time female head coach of a national women's hockey team in the world. Until 1998, she had won every international tournament as coach of the National Team. After Shannon served as assistant coach of the gold medal teams in the 1992 and 1994 World Championships, held in Tampere, Finland, and Lake Placid, New York, respectively, she became head coach. As head coach during Team Canada's domination of the world hockey scene, she has seen four gold medals at the 1995 and 1996 Pacific Rim Championships in San Jose, California, and Richmond, B.C.; the Three Nations

Cup in Ottawa; and the 1997 World Championships in Kitchener, Ontario. Shannon coached Team Canada to a silver medal win in the 1998 Winter Olympic Games.

As for the future of women in hockey, Shannon thinks that anyone who has the skill level and is able to compete in the larger, physical game should be allowed to play in the NHL. "But I'd rather see a professional women's hockey league, one without intentional body checking, where players rely on skills, skating, and stickhandling, so that the women's game stays pure, one of hockey finesse. And I believe that after the 2002 Winter Olympics in Salt Lake City, women's hockey will naturally evolve into a pro league with the help of the NHL."

CHAPTER 8

Official Business

Officials from around the world at the Olympic
Training Camp, Lake Placid, December 1997.

Marina Zenk

IS OFFICIATING FOR YOU?

Even if you're not playing or coaching hockey, there are lots of ways to get involved in the sport. Every league needs on-ice and off-ice officials to help make the game run smoothly.

Are you a person who likes to see a game played fairly? Do you like to count goals, or add up penalty minutes? Then maybe a career as an official is for you. Not only is it a wonderful opportunity to stay involved with the game, but there is also a tremendous level of satisfaction when you know you have officiated a good game.

OFFICIALS AND THEIR RULES

Referee

The referee is the head official, and she has the last word on any decision. She is also the most noticeable: she's the on-ice official who wears the bright red bands on the arms of her black-and-white striped jersey. The referee calls penalties, decides whether goals count or not, and is responsible for the overall conduct and fair play of the game. It takes a bit of work to become a good referee, and a lot of work to become a great one. Contact your local hockey league for information on training opportunities for referees.

Linesmen

Like referees, linesmen are on-ice officials. That means they have to lace up their skates and join the action to do their job. Linesmen are the referees' assistants: they determine if a play is offside, or if a puck has been iced, and keep their eyes open for other problems during the course of the game. At advanced levels, a game is normally officiated by two linesmen and one referee; recreational and minor league games often make do with two on-ice officials — one referee and one linesman.

Timekeeper

An off-ice official, the timekeeper sits at rinkside and oversees the game clock.

Penalty Timekeeper

Another off-ice official, the penalty timekeeper times the penalties assessed by the referees. Often at minor league levels, the timekeeper will also look after penalties.

Goal Judge

The goal judge has the best seat in the house — the one right behind the net. It's her job to watch for the puck to cross the goal line. As soon as it does, she turns on the red light to signal a goal.

Official Scorer

The official scorer has one of the most important off-ice jobs. She gets the line-ups from each team before the game, and keeps track of scoring plays and penalties during a game.

CANADIAN HOCKEY OFFICIATING PROGRAM

The Canadian Hockey Officiating Program (CHOP), operated under the Canadian Hockey Association, offers six levels of referee certification. The level system is the foundation for training and development of amateur hockey officials across Canada. CHOP has opportunities for everyone from initiation at Level I through high performance levels V and VI.

- *Level I* is the basic entry level course for beginners and those sixteen years of age and under. It prepares the novice official for her first minor league hockey assignment.
- *Level II* prepares officials for competitive minor league hockey. Its status further enhances the training skills of minor league hockey officials while preparing them for the next level of responsibility.
- *Level III* prepares officials to be referees or linesmen in competitive minor league hockey playoffs; regional playoffs; women's provincials, regionals, and nationals; and the Canada Winter Games. Level III training also prepares linesmen for Junior B, C, and D; Midget AAA; and Bantam AAA.
- *Level IV* entitles officials to referee international and International Ice Hockey Federation competitions and the women's Olympic competition. They are also prepared to referee Junior B, C, and D; Senior A, B, and C; and minor league hockey provincial championships. In addition, Level IV also prepares officials to be linesmen in Major Junior A, Senior AA, Canadian Interuniversity Athletic Union (CIAU), interbranch, and international championships.

- *Level V* officials are qualified to referee Major Junior A, Junior A, Senior AA, CIAU, and national championships.
- *Level VI* officials are the premier officials in the nation and are qualified to officiate at elite national and world championships.

All referees and officials must upgrade their certification every year through CHOP clinics. There are many different opportunities in officiating; with the right training, you can officiate at national and international competitions, including the Women's World Championships, and at European tournaments. You truly can officiate around the world.

USA HOCKEY OFFICIATING PROGRAM

The USA Hockey Officiating Program has established levels of achievement for each individual, from the beginner to the highly skilled official. Instruction and supportive material are provided on a progressive step-by-step basis so that the official can gradually improve her ability and training.

- *Level I* officials are required to complete an open-book rules exam designed to assist the official in becoming familiar with the many basic playing rules of USA Hockey.
- *Level II* officials have one or two years of experience and are prepared to learn advanced techniques of officiating. Many of the questions that stem from the basics are answered at the second level. Officials at this level are

required to complete an open-book playing rules exam and attend a mandatory pre-season USA Hockey seminar.

- *Level III* officials have proven their abilities over years of officiating. Level III studies include the psychology of officiating and judgment. There is also an open-book playing rules exam, and officials must attend a mandatory pre-season USA Hockey seminar.

- *Level IV* entails officiating at USA Hockey junior, high school, and higher-level games. The level IV official must have two years of experience at level III. Applicants must successfully complete the open-book and closed-book exams, pass an on-ice skating exam, and attend a mandatory pre-season USA Hockey seminar.

PRO FILE

KAREN KOST

Official Official

Karen Kost is another woman who polices the ice, but she's not a coach, or a police officer. Karen is the only female official in Canada to hold a Level V from the Canadian Hockey Officiating Program (CHOP). "Although we like to call ourselves officials, we are namely referees and linesmen."

Karen started playing hockey in Peterborough, Ontario, but didn't begin her officiating career until after she moved to Alberta. "I refereed volleyball through college and university; that's how I made enough money to finish my schooling. You can referee ten to fifteen volleyball games a day, but in hockey you can only do two or three games."

Karen started officiating hockey after she was benched during a championship game in Calgary. "I was playing quite well when the coach suddenly decided to bench me. I took off my helmet and gloves and sat down at the end of the bench. A friend, who was a linesman, came over and encouraged me to take up officiating. At the beginning of the next season, I went to my first referee clinic. I haven't looked back since."

Karen attended a weekend-long clinic, held once a year by CHOP. Although she was the only woman present at her first clinic, she was inspired by the positive response she received from the instructors and officials in attendance. "They were genuinely surprised, but pleased, that I was serious about hockey. Until recently, most of the men officiating at our games weren't as dedicated to the female game as we were."

Karen believes that the key to breaking new ground and changing old attitudes is to progress through the system gradually, learning as much as you possibly can. If you are a confident and experienced official, you may also be selected to become an instructor. Karen has finished her seventh season as one of the few female instructors in Canada, and almost two decades as an official.

Most recently, she officiated at the European Championships in Russia in March 1996, then went on to the World Training Camp in Barcelona, Spain, in preparation for the 1998 Winter Olympic Games. Karen has officiated several World Championships, and has formed friendships with many of the officials and players. "The World Championships are like going home again."

Karen had the opportunity to officiate during one of the Canada–U.S. pre-Olympic series games, played in Calgary's impressive Saddledome. The attendance of 15,194 spectators was a world record, although it was one of the rare instances that Canada lost (1–3). Karen felt overwhelmed by the tide of support building for Canada. As always, she was at the top of her game. "You have to know the rules of the game; you have to be confident, outgoing, and stand out as a proven leader."

Does Karen think there will be a female referee in the NHL? "Yes, I believe there could be a female referee in the NHL someday, but perhaps not as a linesman. One of the key aspects of being a linesman in the NHL is breaking up fights. Women may not be physically strong enough for that."

Karen hopes that more women will get involved in officiating and instructing. "Positive reinforcement of women in hockey — playing, coaching, officiating, you name it — will make it second nature to associate women with the game."

Karen is the head instructor for the officiating program at the Shooting Star Hockey School in Stettler, Alberta. If you'd like more information, you can call (403) 884-2393.

PRO FILE

MARGOT PAGE

Official Coach

Margot started playing hockey in the same way as countless other youngsters in Canada — on a frozen lake near her home. She grew up in several small communities, including New Liskeard, Ontario, which is one hundred miles north of North Bay. "It was always cold and hockey was something to do after school. Everyone played."

Since there wasn't a girls' team in New Liskeard, Margot enrolled in track and field, but didn't forget about playing hockey. Margot found a team to play for and soon became a member of one of Canada's top-ranked senior women's teams, the Aeros. A veteran of three National teams, 1990, 1992, and 1994, Margot also played for the Mississauga Chiefs (1994–1996) and the Aeros from 1989 to 1994. She was named the Central Ontario Women's Hockey League (COWHL) most valuable player from 1992 to 1995.

Margot was recently selected as the first head coach of Niagara University's women's hockey team. So far, she's been busy planning and developing a program at the New York university. Margot is looking forward to building a reputable team, which begins its first season in 1998. "I've recruited most of the players from Buffalo and southern Ontario, where there is a strong emphasis on hockey."

Margot always wanted to be a coach, and the position at Niagara University seemed like the perfect opportunity. She also serves as strength and conditioning coach for the entire athletic program. "It's the ideal situation for me, I'm doing something I love, the commute isn't bad, and women's hockey will be a big part of this university."

On top of her coaching duties, Margot also served as expert analyst and color analyst for women's hockey on TSN in 1997–1998, and for the CBC at the 1998 Olympic Games.

CHAPTER 9

The Girls of Winter

The Lady Blues, University of Toronto team, 1997–98.

K. Hughes

WOMEN'S HOCKEY AROUND THE WORLD

When women's hockey became an Olympic sport in 1998, and with the World Championships attracting more and more attention, the popularity of women's hockey skyrocketed. And why not? Our game has as much action, finesse, and skill as any other. Canadian women's hockey programs have grown almost 400 percent since the first World Championships in 1990, and U.S. women's hockey registration has seen an increase of over 250 percent since the 1990–1991 season.

Beatrice Foods, a Canadian corporation, became the first major sponsor of a women's hockey team when it provided $500,000 of funding to the Toronto Aeros, now called the Beatrice Aeros, in 1998. Barry Hogan, vice-president of Beatrice Foods, believes women's hockey will continue to be the darling of the Winter Olympic Games. "It's clean, healthy, and wholesome: it's what sport is supposed to be."

Canada and the United States lead the world in producing top-ranked hockey players, but women everywhere enjoy the sport. More than twenty countries have national women's hockey teams, and that number is growing all the time. Here's a quick look at women's hockey around the world.

- North America: Canada, United States.
- Europe: Sweden, Russia, Finland, Norway, Switzerland, Germany, Denmark, Belgium, Latvia, Czech Republic, Slovakia, France, Netherlands, Great Britain, Ukraine, Austria, Italy, Scotland.
- Asia: China, Japan, Korea, Kazakhstan.
- Other Countries: Australia, South Africa.

United States

The U.S. team, gold medal winners at the 1998 Winter Olympic games in Nagano, Japan, were consistent silver medalists in the 1990, 1992, 1994, and 1997 World Championships, the 1995 and 1996 Pacific Rim Championships, and the 1996 Three Nations Cup. The second Three Nations Cup, in December 1997, saw Team USA finally take first place over Canada, a sign of things to come. Their highly motivated, skilled, and determined team captured Olympic gold in a fantastic finale. Team USA has numerous first-rate, dedicated players who have somehow managed to beat the odds — the U.S., until now, has had poorly managed women's hockey programs. Nineteen ninety-eight was their make or break year, and the stiff competition did not deter the talents of the players, who rose above expectations and stole the podium from the long-standing undisputed champions of the world — Canada. The Olympics gave a tremendous boost to women's hockey, and preparations are already underway for the 2002 Winter Olympic Games in Salt Lake City, Utah.

China

China didn't have a team in 1987, but by 1990 they were planning their rise; they sent observers to videotape the first World Championships. Through extensive training, they established a women's hockey team that was good enough to be the Asian representative at the 1992, 1994, and 1997 World Championships! At present, China may be perceived as becoming a hockey hotbed, since the national women's team is ranked fourth in the world. However, they do well because they train a small group of players year-round. To date, they have fewer than two hundred women playing in the whole country. The Chinese women traditionally play a patient game and rely heavily on goaltending to keep them in contention. After finishing fourth in the 1994 and 1997 Women's World Championships, and third in the 1995 and 1996 Pacific Rim Championships, they appear to be getting stronger and improving their skills, but they still rely on two or three forwards to do the bulk of their scoring. They are a team that demanded attention during what they saw as a chance to improve their country's image — the Olympic Games in 1998, where they placed an impressive fourth.

Denmark

The level of play is rapidly improving in this small European country. Team Denmark finished fourth in the 1989 European Championships, and managed a third-place finish in the following year. This team made its first appearance at the World Championships in 1992, where they placed seventh. Denmark currently competes in the European B Championships, where they won the gold in 1996, enabling them to compete in the European A Championships. An impressive showing from a country that boasts only four hundred players.

Finland

Team Finland is the European powerhouse. In the 1992 European Championships, Team Finland won all games, outscoring its opposition 73–2! In the 1992, 1994, and 1997 World Championships, they finished third. Finland won the gold medal at the 1989, 1991, 1993, and 1995 European A Championships. The 1996 European Championships gave Finland a bronze medal, qualifying them for the 1997 World Championships, where they took home yet another bronze medal. Team Finland debuted in the 1998 Olympic Games as the third seed, but as recently as 1997 they tied Team USA in second place at the World Championships. They have a strong defensive line and rely on the speed of their forwards to make their opponents sweat. Finland will always make the most of every opportunity to score. Not surprisingly, they brought home the bronze medal from the 1998 Winter Olympics.

Germany

Women's hockey in Germany has grown by leaps and bounds since the first team was formed in Bavaria in 1974. The first official women's hockey league was formed eight years later, in 1982, by former International Ice Hockey Federation president Dr. Gunther Sabetzki. They competed in the 1989 European A Championships, where they won the bronze medal. In 1994, Germany participated in the World Championships, where they placed eighth. Unfortunately, they failed to qualify for the 1997 World Championships, losing the opportunity to compete in the 1998 Olympic Games.

Japan

The first women's hockey team in Japan was formed in Tokyo in 1973. Now, women's hockey is played all over the country. In 1981, the Japan Ice Hockey Federation hosted the first official women's National Championships. By 1990, Team Japan was the Asian representative at the World Championships, where they placed seventh. Japan was fourth at both Pacific Rim Championships in 1995 and 1996. They came in second at the 1996 Asian Championships, losing to China but defeating Kazakhstan 6–2. As host country, Japan received an automatic entry into the 1998 Olympic Games, but their national women's hockey team has not qualified for the World Championships since 1990. Japan played with great pride at the Olympics, but unfortunately their skills were not good enough to make them serious contenders for any of the top three medals. They played well, but despite their determination, they placed sixth.

Sweden

Women's hockey teams have existed in Sweden since 1969. This depth of experience shows on the international level; Team Sweden has won several bronze medals at the European Championships, and finished fourth at the 1990 and 1992 World Championships. Annica Ahlen of Team Sweden was named top goaltender in the 1992 series, and was also the youngest Swedish athlete to participate on a national team — at 15 years old. Team Sweden won the silver and gold medals at the 1995 and 1996 European Championships, respectively. Sweden placed in the top five at the 1997 World Championships to qualify for its Olympic debut in Nagano, Japan. Team Sweden is a mature group of athletes who have played at the top level of the game. They are technically sound, but rely more on goaltending rather than on offensive attacks, which keeps their game scores low. They placed fifth at the Winter Olympic Games in Nagano.

Switzerland

Swiss women have only been playing organized hockey since 1980, but they've already made an impact on the international scene with strong finishes at both European Championships. Although the sport grew very slowly, the first hockey camp for girls was held in 1983, and 1984 saw the official admission of women's hockey in the Swiss Ice Hockey Federation. The Schweizer Cup, the first international tournament in 1989, had teams from Germany, France, Italy, and Switzerland competing. Switzerland won the bronze medal at the 1995 European A Championships, and qualified to attend the World Championships held in 1990, 1992, 1994, and 1997, where they placed sixth, eighth, and seventh twice, respectively. The Swiss women's hockey program experienced a noticeable improvement when they started to sign players from the U.S., Canada, and Finland to play on their teams. It boosts the level of play, and therefore helps the Swiss players improve.

Norway

Norway qualified to attend the first four Women's World Championships, in 1990, 1992, 1994, and 1997, by finishing in the top five teams at the European A Championships. They placed fourth at the 1995 and 1996 European Championships, and sixth and eighth at the 1994 and 1997 World Championships. All this despite the fact that in 1997 they still had only twenty ice rinks in a country of four million people. Norway is the third Scandinavian country with women's hockey, but it is still on a neophyte level. The top sport there is soccer, and the first female hockey teams weren't formed until 1987. In 1988, the annual Nordic Cup was launched, with teams from Denmark, Germany, and Switzerland participating.

Russia

Russia placed second in the 1996 European A Championships, although they didn't start competing internationally until 1994. They toured North America to gain experience, and won the gold medal the first time they competed in the European B Championships. They won silver at the 1996 European A Championships, and placed sixth in their first year at the 1997 World Championships. Long considered a "hockey mecca" for men, Russia provided very little support for their fledgling women's team. The difficult beginnings for the Russian team seem to be behind them, and future Olympic status may create the much-needed funding and attention the sport deserves. While they failed to secure a berth for the 1998 Olympic Games, that may make them work all the harder for 2002.

Latvia

Latvia won the European B Championships in 1993, and the silver medal at the 1996 European B Championships in Slovakia.

Belgium

Although Belgium does not compete internationally, they have a joint Dutch/Belgian women's league. Starting in the 1995 season, the Holland and Belgium teams joined to play in one league.

Great Britain

Great Britain currently competes in the European B Championships, where they placed seventh in 1995, and eighth in 1996. Women's hockey in Great Britain was initially an upper-class sport, the only participants being ladies who learned to play while at finishing school in Switzerland. The two varsity teams are from Oxford and Cambridge universities. There is a dearth of players; in

1995 there were only 338 female players registered. There are now two Scottish teams and one Welsh team.

Slovakia

Slovakia currently competes in the European B Championships, where they placed fourth in 1995 and 1996.

France

France placed fifth at the European B Championships in 1995 and 1996.

Netherlands

In 1987, Team Holland traveled to Canada to compete in the first Women's World Hockey Tournament. An official National Women's Team was formed a year later, in 1988. The Dutch National Women's Team has not yet qualified for the World Championships, and finished sixth in the European B Championships in 1995 and 1996. The availability of ice time is the main difficulty in developing female hockey in the Netherlands.

TEAM CANADA

Until recently, Team Canada was the undisputed leader in women's hockey, with gold medal victories in all the World Championships — 1990 (Ottawa, Ontario), 1992 (Tampere, Finland), 1994 (Lake Placid, New York), and 1997 (Kitchener, Ontario) — as well as two golds in the Pacific Rim Championships

Lisa Jiles

The 1998 Canadian Women's Olympic Hockey Team.

— 1995 (San Jose, California) and 1996 (Vancouver, British Columbia) — and a gold in the 1996 Three Nations Cup (Ottawa, Ontario). This dominance reflects Canada's long-standing tradition of women's hockey, and a development system that is constantly improving.

Over thirty thousand players are registered on women's teams across Canada, and the numbers are growing. This kind of support, says Glynis Peters, manager of the female hockey program for the Canadian Hockey Association, ensures that Canada will remain a force in hockey for years to come. "The future looks bright. We offer player development from an early age, and encourage high levels of competition at every level. Now, there are national championships for senior players, and also for younger players, eighteen and under. We are working to ensure that women's hockey develops in a healthy, positive, and safe manner."

Being the best also comes with a certain amount of responsibility. As Glynis says, Canada's hockey organization is striving to be a leader both on and off the ice. "We are trying to take the lead internationally as a good role model for other countries currently developing women's hockey programs."

The next decade promises to be an exciting one for young hockey players in Canada and around the world. There will be many opportunities to travel and meet new friends, to grow as a hockey player, and as a person... so what are you waiting for? It's time you tried women's hockey, the hottest game in town!

TEAM USA

Women have been playing organized hockey in the United States for decades, and in the last twenty-five years the sport has blossomed, especially at the collegiate level. The United States Women's National Team was officially launched in 1990 at the inaugural Women's World Championships.

Without a doubt, the U.S. now has one of the best hockey programs in the world. Just consider their consistent silver medal finishes at the World Championships in 1990, 1992, 1994, and 1997. They also took home silver medals for their outstanding performance in the 1995 and 1996 Pacific Rim Championships.

Tom Kimmel Photography

The 1998 American Women's Olympic Hockey Team.

And again, a silver finish at the inaugural Three Nations Cup in 1996, and for the first time, a gold at the second Three Nations Cup in 1997. It must have been a premonition, because later that season Team USA delivered enough punch to capture the first gold medal in women's hockey at the 1998 Winter Olympic Games. Quite an accomplishment.

The first World Championships in 1990 was one of the biggest highlights for the team, as coach Karen Kay recalls. "Never in my life did I expect to see ten thousand people at a women's hockey game; you always hope for that kind of turnout, but don't expect it. Every player took home that experience and exposure."

Karen was assistant coach in 1990, and her subsequent promotion marked the first time a woman has been head coach of Team USA. "It's exciting. And it's about time we had a female hockey coach for the National Team. I only hope I can be a positive role model for younger players and coaches."

The U.S. national program is being updated and improved. In the past, many of the available players were registered on boys' teams, and many others didn't know about the various programs for women. During the 1990–1991 season, 5,573 female hockey players registered with USA Hockey. Since then, that number has increased more than fourfold with over twenty-four thousand registered girls and women playing hockey across the United States today. While the number of girls' and women's teams has increased (from 149 in 1990 to 910 in 1996), the majority of players continue to register on mixed-gender teams.

AWARDS

Besides the excitement, prestige, and thrill of winning a hockey game, there is also the chance to receive awards. Apart from the gold, silver, and bronze medals awarded during the Olympic Games and the World Championships, Canada offers its own recognition to the top teams of the year. The Esso Women's National Hockey Championships provides the winning teams with three cups. The gold medal winner receives the Abby Hoffman Cup, the second-place team is awarded the Fran Rider Cup, and the third-place team receives the Maureen McTeer Cup. And every team has the chance to win the Most Sportsmanlike Team award, the Mickey Walker Cup. A more recent award for individual performance is the

Athlete Achievement Award which recognizes a special athlete.

The Patty Kazmaier Memorial Award is an American national-level award designed to recognize the accomplishments of the most outstanding player in women's intercollegiate ice hockey. The first award, presented to the player who represents the highest standards of personal and team excellence, was given to Brandy Fisher on April 1, 1998, in Boston, Massachusetts, at Madison Square Gardens. Brandy is a forward at the University of New Hampshire, and is one of the highest scorers in women's intercollegiate varsity hockey.

The American Women's College Hockey Alliance (AWCHA) recently announced a national championship for women's intercollegiate hockey. The first-ever AWCHA Division I National Hockey Championship was held at Boston's FleetCenter, Massachusetts, in March 1998. The top-seeded University of New Hampshire defeated Brown University 4–1.

CANADA'S 1998 WOMEN'S OLYMPIC TEAM

No.	Goaltender	Hometown
30	Lesley Reddon	Fredericton, New Brunswick
33	Manon Rhéaume	Charlesbourg, Quebec

Defense

4	Becky Kellar	Hagarsville, Ontario
6	Thérèse Brisson	Fredericton, New Brunswick
9	Fiona Smith	Edam, Saskatchewan
21	Judy Diduck	Sherwood Park, Alberta
77	Cassie Campbell	Brampton, Ontario
91	Geraldine Heaney	Weston, Ontario

Forwards

3	France St. Louis	St.Hubert, Quebec
7	Jennifer Botterill	Winnipeg, Manitoba
12	Lori Dupuis	Williamstown, Ontario
14	Kathy McCormack	Fredericton, New Brunswick
15	Danielle Goyette	St. Nazaire, Quebec
16	Jayna Hefford	Kingston, Ontario
17	Stacy Wilson	Moncton, New Brunswick
18	Nancy Drolet	Drummondville, Quebec
22	Hayley Wickenheiser	Calgary, Alberta

27	Laura Schuler	Scarborough, Ontario
61	Vicky Sunohara	Scarborough, Ontario
89	Karen Nystrom	Scarborough, Ontario

Coaches

Team Leader	Glynis Peters	Calgary, Alberta
Head Coach	Shannon Miller	Calgary, Alberta
Assistant Coach	Daniele Sauvageau	St. Eustache, Quebec
Assistant Coach	Ray Bennett	Red Deer, Alberta
Assistant Coach	Clare Drake	Edmonton, Alberta

TEAM CANADA

Jennifer Botterill
Forward

At seventeen years old, Jennifer was the youngest member of the 1998 Olympic Team. In 1995, she played with the Winnipeg Storm, the Senior Women's Provincial Champions. By 1996, she was training at the Olympic Oval high performance female hockey program in Calgary. The 1997–1998 women's Olympic Team training camp was her first involvement with the National Team. Jennifer played for the defending champion, the Alberta Oval team, during the seventeenth annual National Championships held in March 1998 in Calgary, when they defeated the North York Beatrice Aeros by a score of 3–2 in the first period of overtime.

Thérèse Brisson
Defense

Thérèse has an impressive hockey background. She was Concordia University's Female Rookie of the Year in 1986 and was twice named Female Athlete of the Year in 1988 and 1989. Thérèse has several gold medals so far; she played for Team Quebec when they won the 1994 National Championships and the 1995 Esso Women's Nationals, where she was named Most Valuable Defense. She also won gold with Team Canada at the 1996 Pacific Rim Championships, the 1996 Three Nations Cup, and the 1994 and 1997 World Championships. Thérèse is currently playing for Team New Brunswick, which placed fifth in the 1998

Nationals, where she won the Most Valuable Defense award. Thérèse was the second-highest scorer in the 1998 Olympics with five goals and two assists.

Cassie Campbell

Defense

Cassie played for Team Ontario at the 1991 Canada Winter Games, and from 1992 to 1996 she was an integral member of Guelph University's varsity team, the Gryphons. She played at the 1995 and 1996 Pacific Rim Championships, winning two gold medals. She was a gold medalist for her part in the 1996 Three Nations Cup. She also has two more gold medals from the 1994 and 1997 Women's World Championships. Add to that a silver Olympic medal, and Cassie's collection is almost finished. In the 1998 Winter Olympics, Cassie scored one goal and had two assists. She is currently playing for the Beatrice Aeros, which represented Ontario at the Nationals in March 1998 when they won the silver medal.

Judy Diduck

Defense

Judy was a four-time gold medalist for Team Canada at the 1990, 1992, 1994, and 1997 Women's World Championships. In the 1994 series she had six assists in five games. Add another three gold medals from the 1996 Three Nations Cup and both Pacific Rim Championships in 1995 and 1996, and you have an impressive hockey career. Judy learned her craft with her brother, Gerald, who currently plays in the NHL with the Phoenix Coyotes. From 1985 to 1998, she participated in every National Championships with the Edmonton Chimos. In

1998 the Chimos won the bronze medal after defeating Team Quebec 4–2. Judy scored two goals and two assists in the 1998 Winter Olympics.

Nancy Drolet
Forward

Nancy was named Junior Athlete of the Year in 1993 by the Sports Federation of Canada, in the same month that *Inside Hockey* named her the "Next Great Women's Player." Nancy started playing hockey by age four. Her natural talent and her uncanny sense of the game make her one of the best players around. By age seventeen, she was playing for the Quebec Junior Team, which won the bronze medal at the Canada Winter Games. Nancy was an integral member of Team Canada for their 1992, 1994, and 1997 wins at the World Championships. In the 1997 series she scored four goals and two assists in five games, and scored three goals in the final, including the game winner in overtime! She made room for two more gold medals in 1996 for her work at the Three Nations Cup and the Pacific Rim Championships. During the 1998 Winter Olympics, Nancy scored one goal and two assists. After her Olympic stint, she returned home to practice with the All-Star team from Quebec in preparation for the Nationals, where they placed fourth.

Lori Dupuis
Forward

Lori is a relative newcomer to Team Canada, finding her place on the winning team in the 1995 and 1996 Pacific Rim Championships. In the 1997 World

Championships, she had two goals and four assists in five games. Lori scored two goals and one assist in the 1998 Winter Olympics. She currently plays with the University of Toronto.

Danielle Goyette

Forward

Danielle's speedy skates earned her a spot on the National Team during its gold streak at the 1992, 1994, and 1997 World Championships. In the 1994 series she was point leader with nine goals and three assists. She was also named to the 1994 All-Star team and to the 1995 Pacific Rim All-Star team. Danielle was top-scorer and Canadian point leader in the 1998 Winter Olympics with eight goals and one assist. Danielle, a proven sharpshooter, competed in the 1998 Nationals with Team Quebec, with a fourth place finish.

Geraldine Heaney

Defense

Geraldine has always set her sights high. Besides being recognized by *Inside Hockey* as one of the top female players in the world, she is most often remembered for her winning goal at the 1990 World Championships in Ottawa. Geraldine scored two goals and four assists in the 1998 Winter Olympic which put her in the top three point leaders. She has won gold after gold for her participation in all of the Women's World Championships from 1987 to 1997. In 1992 Geraldine was named to the All-Star team and earned the Directorate Award for best defense, and in 1994 again won the Directorate Award for best defense. And she is the only woman to be featured in *Hockey Night in Canada*'s top 10 goals for the 1989–1990 season. She is an advisory member of Louisville Hockey, where her input helps develop female hockey equipment. Geraldine played in the 1998 Nationals as an eighteen-year veteran on the Beatrice Aeros, when they won the silver medal.

Jayna Hefford
Forward

Jayna has only recently come to play hockey with the National Team. In 1995, she was playing with the Ottawa Regional Select Team, an under-eighteen team, but by 1996, she had been named OWIAA Rookie of the Year for the University of Toronto. Jayna has a gold under her belt for her participation in the 1993 Under-18 Nationals with Team Ontario, as well as three gold and four silver medals for the OWHA Provincial Championships from 1988 to 1996. Jayna scored one goal in the 1998 Winter Olympics.

Becky Kellar
Defense

The 1997–1998 Olympic Team training camp was Becky's first involvement with the National Team. She played with the Brown University Bears from 1993 to 1997, and won several All-Ivy awards. Becky scored one goal and had two assists in the 1998 Winter Olympics. She was signed to play for the Beatrice Aeros, who represented Team Ontario at the 1998 Nationals.

Kathy McCormack
Forward

Kathy's previous experience with Team Canada was at the 1993 U.S. Olympic Festival in San Antonio, Texas. From 1991 to 1997 she played Senior A female hockey in New Brunswick with the Maritime Sports Blades. Kathy represented Team New Brunswick at the 1998 Nationals in Calgary, where the Maritime Sports Blades All-Stars placed fifth.

Karen Nystrom
Forward

Karen is a natural athlete. During high school she was named most valuable player in soccer and hockey (1984–1989) and received the Outstanding Achievement Award in 1988 and Athlete of the Year in 1989. She was the recipient of a full hockey scholarship to Northeastern University in Boston, but came home to play in three World Championships, in 1992, 1994, and 1997. Karen has two more gold medals from the 1996 Pacific Rim Championships and the Three Nations Cup. From 1988 to 1997 Karen was named to the OWHA All-Star team every year. Karen scored one goal in the 1998 Winter Olympics.

Lesley Reddon
Goaltender

Lesley's goaltending career took off when she was OWIAA Champion with the University of Toronto Lady Blues for four seasons from 1989 to 1993. She was a Senior AA Champion with the Toronto Aeros, and a gold medalist at the 1991

Nationals. In 1995, Lesley was the first woman to play men's CIAU hockey with the University of New Brunswick Reds. She played at the 1994 and 1997 World Championships, as well as the 1995 Pacific Rim Championships, where she received the Outstanding Goalkeeper Award and was named to the tournament All-Star team. In 1997, Lesley backstopped Canada to a thrilling overtime victory over Team USA in the gold medal final of the World Championships. Her position on the Olympic Team came by perseverance, hard work, and determination. Plus, she's a great goaltender! Lesley played for Team New Brunswick at the 1998 Nationals.

Manon Rhéaume
Goaltender

The world's most recognized female goalie has an impressive public career that has brought women's hockey into the media limelight since 1990. Besides being the first Canadian woman to play in an NHL exhibition game, with the Tampa Bay Lightning in 1995, Manon is also a dedicated National Team member. Manon backstopped during the 1992 and 1994 World Championships, as well as the 1996 Pacific Rim Championships. In 1992 she earned a 0.67 goals-against average and was named to the All-Star team; in 1994 she earned a 1.72 goals-against average and was again named to the All-Star team. It was a tough decision to try out for the Olympic Team, as it meant Manon had to put her professional career on hold — she was netminder for the West Coast Hockey League's Reno Renegades — to try to earn a much-coveted spot. She had failed to make the cut for the 1997 World Championships, and there was no guarantee she'd make this team after giving up her pro hockey career — and her salary. Back-stopping men's hockey is a different game, and Manon had to make several adjustments to make the Olympic Team.

Laura Schuler
Forward
From 1989 to 1994, Laura played with the Northeastern University Huskies in Boston on a full athletic scholarship. She played at three World Championships and two Pacific Rim Championships, earning gold medals at all. During the 1990 World Championships, she scored four goals and had two assists in five games. Recently, she has been playing with the Newtonbrook Panthers and the University of Toronto Blues.

Fiona Smith
Defense
From 1993 to 1997 Fiona played hockey for the Edmonton Chimos; the 1997 season was gold for Fiona and her team at the Esso Women's Nationals. She played in the 1995 and 1996 Pacific Rim Championships, and in the 1997 World Championships. As a member of the defending champions, the Edmonton Chimos, Fiona plays alongside one of her Olympian teammates, Judy Diduck. The Edmonton Chimos won the bronze medal at the 1998 Nationals in Calgary, Alberta. Fiona scored one goal in the 1998 Winter Olympics.

Vicky Sunohara

Forward

Vicky was on the gold-medal winning women's team at the 1990 and 1997 World Championships. In 1990 she scored six goals and had three assists in five games. She also played for Team Canada when they won gold at the 1996 Three Nations Cup in Ottawa. In her 1987 season while playing in the Scarborough hockey league, Vicky was named NCAA Championships Rookie of the Year. From 1987 to 1990, Vicky was named to the All-American All-Star Team while attending Northeastern University. In 1991 she was the University of Toronto Rookie of the Year. She played with the Blues from 1990 to 1994, as well as with the Scarborough Firefighters. She won the bronze medal at the Esso Women's Nationals with one of her teams, the North York Aeros; her other team was the Newtonbrook Panthers. Vicky also instructs hockey. She played for the silver-winning Team Ontario at the 1998 Nationals, where she donned her Beatrice Aeros uniform. Vicky scored one goal and three assists in the 1998 Winter Olympics.

France St. Louis

Forward

France is my choice as athlete of the decade for Canada! She was named Quebec's Athlete of the Decade, 1980–1990, while playing lacrosse, and was a member of the National Lacrosse Team from 1985 to 1989. She was named Quebec's Athlete of the Year in 1986. And the list of hockey awards is endless:

- 1988, 1989, and 1990 National Championships gold medalist
- 1988, 1989, and 1990 Most Valuable Player at Nationals

- 1990 Quebec Ice Hockey Federation Athlete of the Year
- 1991, 1992, and 1993 Most Valuable Player in Quebec Senior A League
- 1994 Quebec IHF Athlete of the Year
- 1994, 1995, and 1996 gold medalist at Esso Women's Nationals with Team Quebec
- 1997 silver medalist at Esso Women's Nationals with Team Quebec
- 1997 Most Valuable Player and Top Scorer in Quebec Senior A League

France played in the 1990, 1992, 1994, and 1997 World Championships, competing at the 1997 Worlds with a cast on her broken wrist. France was captain of Team Canada at the 1992 and 1994 Worlds. She also brought home the gold from the 1996 Three Nations Cup and the 1996 Pacific Rim Championships. France won the most valuable player championship award in the 1998 Nationals with Team Quebec; she also scored one goal and two assists at the 1998 Winter Olympics.

Hayley Wickenheiser
Forward

Hayley was only eleven when she watched the first Women's World Championships in 1990, and she knew then that hockey would be a big part of her life. She had already been playing the game for six years, with her dad coaching her minor league team in Calgary. Hayley is considered to be the "next generation" of hockey players, women who have the skill, finesse, toughness, and ability to be a professional hockey player, and she is undoubted one of the top players in the country today. Hayley played on the gold medal team at the 1994 and 1997

World Championships; she was only fifteen in 1994 when she won her first gold medal, and at the 1997 Worlds she racked up an impressive four goals and five assists in five games. Hayley also participated in the 1995 and 1996 Pacific Rim Championships, as well as the 1996 Three Nations Cup. The explosive Hayley played for the Alberta Oval team at the 1998 Nationals when they won the gold medal. At the 1998 Winter Olympics Hayley scored one goal and six assists, placing her in the top three point-leaders. More recently, Hayley was invited to the Philadelphia Flyers' hockey camp by Head Coach Bobby Camp.

Stacy Wilson
Forward
Stacy was a three-time National Team member in 1990, 1992, and 1994. She played for Team Canada in the 1995 and 1996 Pacific Rim Championships. Stacy also played for the second-place Maritime Blades in the 1995 National Championships, where she scored six goals and six assists in six games and was named most valuable player. Stacy scored one goal and five assists in the 1998 Winter Olympics.

UNITED STATES 1998 OLYMPIC WOMEN'S TEAM

No.	Goaltender	Hometown
1	Sara DeCosta	Warwick, Rhode Island

29   Sarah Tueting   Winnetka, Illinois

Defense

2   Tara Mounsey   Concord, New Hampshire
4   Angela Ruggiero   Harrison, Michigan
5   Colleen Coyne   East Falmouth, Massachusetts
7   Sue Merz   Greenwich, Connecticut
14   Vicki Movessian   Lexington, Massachusetts
24   Chris Bailey   Marietta, New York

Forwards

3   Lisa Brown-Miller   Union Lake, Michigan
6   Karen Bye   River Falls, Wisconsin
8   Laurie Baker   Concord, Massachusetts
9   Sandra Whyte   Saugus, Massachusetts
11   A.J. Mleczko   Nantucket, Massachusetts
12   Jenny Schmidgall   Edina, Minnesota
15   Shelley Looney   Trenton, Michigan
18   Alana Blahoski   St. Paul, Minnesota
20   Katie King   Salem, New Hampshire
21   Cammi Granato   Downers Grove, Illinois
22   Gretchen Ulion   Marlborough, Connecticut
25   Tricia Dunn   Derry, New Hampshire

Coaches

Team Leader	Amie Hilles	Colorado Springs, Colorado
Head Coach	Ben Smith	Gloucester, Massachusetts
Assistant Coach	Tom Mutch	Canton, Massachusetts

TEAM USA

Chris Bailey

Defense

Chris started playing hockey at the tender age of three, after she saw her cousins wearing all their "cool" equipment. Through determination she eventually became a four-time member of the U.S. Women's National Team in 1994, 1995, 1996, and 1997. Chris was also on the U.S. Women's Select Team in 1993, 1995, 1996, and 1997, and on the 1995 IIHF Pacific Rim Women's Hockey Championships All-Tournament team, and was chosen as the Outstanding Defensive Player. Chris played four years of collegiate hockey at Providence College, where she scored a career total of seventy-three points on twenty-five goals and forty-eight assists in ninety-nine games. She was the top-scoring defender, earned All-Eastern College Athletic Conference honors as a junior and a senior, and was MVP at the 1994 ECAC Championships. Chris plans to finish grad school and coach hockey at the college level. Chris had one assist in the 1998 Winter Olympics.

Laurie Baker
Forward

Laurie made her first appearance on the U.S. Women's National Team in 1997, where she tallied two goals and four assists in five games, the second top scorer in the tournament. Laurie was named the 1997 USA Hockey Women's Player of the Year for her accomplishments with Team USA and Providence College. She was also a member of the 1996 U.S. Select Team, and helped lead the Friars to the ECAC semifinals and was on the ECAC All-Star team the same year. Laurie scored four goals and three assists, making her one of the top scorers in the 1998 Winter Olympics. Laurie plans to coach a young hockey team.

Alana Blahoski
Forward

Alana was a two-time member of the U.S. National Team in 1996 and 1997, and has a record of two goals and four assists in ten games. She was on the Select Team in 1995, 1996, and 1997. Alana was co-captain of the Friars when she was a student at Providence College, finishing her career with eighty-three points on thirty-five goals and forty-eight assists. She was a three-time All-Star in hockey. Alana scored two assists in the 1998 Winter Olympics.

Lisa Brown-Miller
Forward

Lisa has been a member of the U.S. National Team since its inception and is one of just three players to have appeared on all six teams in 1990, 1992, 1994, 1995, 1996, and 1997. In thirty games she had thirteen goals and twenty-five assists, and was also on the Select Team in 1993, 1995, 1996, and 1997. She was named MVP at the 1992 World Championships. Lisa played four years of hockey at Providence College and earned All-Eastern Athletic Conference accolades. She was named ECAC Player of the Year and American Women's Hockey Coaches' Association Player of the Year several times. Lisa scored one goal and one assist in the 1998 Winter Olympics.

Karyn Bye

Forward

Karyn was a five-time member of the U.S. National Team in 1992, 1994, 1995, 1996, and 1997 and has tallied twenty-five goals and twenty assists in twenty-four games. She was also on the U.S. Women's Select Team in 1993, 1995, 1996, and 1997. Karyn was named *USA Today* Athlete of the Month in May 1995 and earned the 1995 USA Hockey Women's Player of the Year Award. She also earned honors and an Outstanding Performance Award for the U.S. at the 1994 World Championships, and competed for Team USA at the U.S. Olympic Festival in San Antonio, Texas, in 1993. Karyn was leading scorer in the 1998 Winter Olympics with five goals and three assists.

Colleen Coyne

Defense

Colleen appeared on five U.S. Women's National Teams (1992, 1994, 1995, 1996, and 1997), and recorded three goals and eleven assists in twenty-four games. She was also a member of the U.S. Select Team in 1993, 1995, 1996, and 1997. Colleen originally started out on a boys' team, then joined the Cape Cod Aces, a girls' team. After finishing high school, Colleen attended the University of New Hampshire (UNH), where her coach convinced her to try out for the National Team. Colleen is a very versatile player who can play just about any position except goal. She played for UNH from 1989 to 1993, was team captain in her senior season, and won two ECAC Championships with the Wildcats.

Sara DeCosta
Goaltender

Sarah made her first appearance on the U.S. Women's National Team at the 1996 Pacific Rim Championships in Richmond, British Columbia, and had played on the 1995 National Junior Team. Sarah completed her freshman season at Providence College in 1997, posting an 18–7–2 record and a 2.66 goals-against average. She was the first girl to play in the Rhode Island Interscholastic League's Championships Division, where she helped Toll Gate reach the title round. She also became the first goalie in 18 years to shut out the Mounties, and earned her team's MVP award.

Tricia Dunn
Forward

Tricia made her first appearance on a U.S. Women's National Team at the 1997 World Championships in Kitchener, Ontario. She had one goal and one assist in five games. She was a member of the Select Team from 1996 to 1997. She also played college hockey with the University of New Hampshire, and won the 1996 ECAC Championships — it took five overtimes, an NCAA record as the longest college game ever played, men's or women's! Tricia scored one goal in the 1998 Winter Olympics.

Cammi Granato

Forward

Cammi is a six-time member of the U.S. Women's National Team (1990, 1992, 1994, 1995, 1996, and 1997). She is one of three players who have been with the team since its inception, and is the all-time leading scorer in the history of the team, with thirty-seven goals and twenty-seven assists in thirty games. She is also one of the most recognized women's hockey players in the world, and one of the best forwards to ever play the game. At the 1997 World Championships, Cammi was the leading scorer with eight points in five games. She also led the U.S. in scoring at the 1996 Pacific Rim Championships with nine points in five games, and was named Outstanding Forward. Cammi was named the 1996 USA Hockey Women's Player of the Year. Cammi was second top-scorer with four goals and four assists in the 1998 Winter Olympics.

Katie King

Forward

Katie made her first appearance on the U.S. Women's National Team at the 1997 World Championships, where she recorded two goals and one assist. She was also a member of the U.S. Select Team in 1995 and 1996. In her senior year at Brown University in Massachusetts, she was named the 1996 ECAC Player of the Year as well as the Ivy League Player of the Year for the third consecutive year! Katie scored four goals and four assists in the 1998 Winter Olympics.

Shelley Looney

Forward

Shelley was a five-time member of the U.S. Women's National Team (1992, 1994, 1995, 1996, and 1997). She has recorded sixteen goals and sixteen assists in twenty-five games. Shelley was also a member of the Select team in 1993, 1995, 1996, and 1997. She won an Outstanding Performance Award at the 1997 World Championships and at the 1995 Pacific Rim Championships. While a junior at Northeastern University, she was named Most Valuable Player at the ECAC Championships, and in her senior year she was named ECAC Player of the Year. Shelley scored four goals and one assist in the 1998 Winter Olympics.

Sue Merz

Defense

Sue is another five-time member of the U.S. Women's National Team (1990, 1992, 1994, 1995, and 1996), where she recorded six goals and ten assists in twenty-five games. She also appeared on the Select Team in 1993, 1995, 1996, and 1997. Sue was only nineteen when she competed with Team USA at the U.S. Olympic Festival in 1993. She played defense for her college team from 1990 to 1994, and was named to the All-Eastern College Athletic Conference and the New England Hockey Writers All-Star team. When she finished her career at the University of New Hampshire, she had totalled 103 points on 50 goals and 53 assists. Sue also played hockey overseas for SC Lyss of the Swiss National League. Sue scored one goal and five assists in the 1998 Winter Olympics.

A.J. Mleczko

Forward

Allison Jamie, or A.J. to her friends, has appeared on three U.S. Women's National Teams in 1995, 1996, and 1997. She had three goals and seven assists in fifteen games, and was a member of the U.S. Women's Select Team in 1995, 1996, and 1997. At Harvard University, she finished the 1996 season with forty-two points on twenty-six goals and sixteen assists, and established herself as Harvard's all-time leading scorer with 143 points. A.J. was Harvard's lone All-Eastern College Athletic Conference selection in 1994, and her thirty-four goals and fifty-one points broke the Harvard record for goals in a season. A.J. scored two goals and two assists in the 1998 Winter Olympics.

Tara Mounsey

Defense

Tara has appeared on two U.S. Women's National Teams in 1996 and 1997. She was named U.S. Player of the Game at the 1997 Women's World Championships after Team USA's 6–0 win against China. She earned an Outstanding Performance Award at the 1996 Pacific Rim Championships, and made the Select Team in 1995 and 1996. In 1995, she was a member of the U.S. Women's National Junior Team. Tara plays for Brown University; in her 1996 season she was named ECAC Rookie of the Year and was named to the ECAC All-Star team. She was the 1996–1997 Ivy League Rookie of the Year, and while in high school she won the New Hampshire Player of the Year, the only girl to ever win that award. Tara scored two goals and four assists in the 1998 Winter Olympics.

Vicki Movsessian

Defense

Vicki started out figure skating, but quickly decided her brother was having more fun playing hockey. She has been playing since she was six years old. Her dedication earned her a four-time spot on the U.S. Women's National Team (1994, 1995, 1996, and 1997), as well as on the U.S. Women's Select Team from 1993 to 1997. Vicki graduated magna cum laude from Providence College in 1994, where she earned All-Eastern College Athletic Conference honors, and was named to the New England Hockey Writers All-Star team. Vicki scored one goal in the 1998 Winter Olympics.

Angela Ruggiero

Defense

Angela was a two-time member of the U.S. Women's National Team in 1996 and 1997 and the U.S. Women's National Junior Team in 1995 and 1996, as well as a three-time U.S. Select Team member in 1995, 1996, and 1997. In 1995 she established a single-season record for goals (forty-two) and points (sixty-three). Angela was the recipient of her school's Greatest Contribution to Sports Award in 1995.

Jenny Schmidgall

Forward

Jenny made her first appearance on the U.S. Women's National Team in 1997, and previously played on two junior teams in 1995 and 1996. Although she is a relative newcomer to hockey — she didn't start playing until the eighth grade in Edina, Michigan — Jenny is a dedicated athlete. Jenny scored two goals and three assists in the 1998 Winter Olympics.

Sarah Tueting

Goaltender

Sarah made her first appearance on an elite-level women's team as a member of the 1996 Select Team at the Three Nations Cup in Ottawa, Ontario. She also played in the 1997 Women's World Championships, making three saves. Sarah played for two years at Dartmouth College, where she was named Ivy League Rookie of the Year and Dartmouth's Rookie of the Year in 1994, in addition to earning All-Eastern College Athletic Conference and All-Ivy honors. Sarah posted an impressive 4–0 gold-medal win in the 1998 Winter Olympics.

Gretchen Ulion

Forward

Gretchen, or Greta to her friends, has played on three U.S. Women's National Teams in 1994, 1995, and 1997, where she recorded nine goals and fifteen assists in fifteen games. She was also on four U.S. Women's Select Teams in 1993, 1995, 1996, and 1997, and competed for Team USA at the U.S. Olympic Festival in 1993 in San Antonio, Texas. In her senior year at Dartmouth College, she had eighty-five points on forty-nine goals and thirty-six assists. She set eleven Dartmouth and four Ivy League records, led Dartmouth to the Ivy League Championships in 1991 and 1993, was twice named Ivy League Player of the Year in 1993 and 1994, and was the Ivy League Rookie of the Year as a freshman.

Greta scored three goals and five assists in the 1998 Winter Olympics, including one goal and one assist in the final gold-medal game.

Sandra Whyte

Forward

Sandra is a five-time member of the U.S. Women's National Team (1992, 1994, 1995, 1996, and 1997), and appeared on the U.S. Women's Select Team in 1993, 1995, 1996, and 1997. Sandra recorded seven goals and eight assists in twenty-five games. She currently stands as Harvard's second all-time leading scorer. She was named Ivy League Player of the Year for both the 1990 and 1991 seasons, and earned the ECAC Player of the Year honors for the 1990–1991 season. Sandra scored two goals and two assists in the 1998 Winter Olympics, including one goal and two assists in the final gold-medal game.

CONCLUSION

After the Game

Women's hockey is developing in leaps and bounds, and the future certainly looks bright. There is something exciting and thrilling to look forward to every year: we've had the Olympic Games in Nagano, Japan, in 1998, and there will be the 1999 World Championships in Finland, the 2000 World Championships in Canada, the 2001 World Championships in the U.S.A., and the 2002 Olympic Games in Salt Lake City, Utah. And a women's professional hockey league will not be far behind.

If you're serious about hockey, you have numerous options. You can play for your high school, college, university, provincial, national, Olympic, or professional team. Once considered a men's sport, women's hockey may one day become as big as the NHL.

Women's hockey is an exciting and dynamic game that can be played at the recreational or competitive level. There is still some controversy surrounding the no intentional body checking rule in women's hockey, but if you prefer to check, you can play in a men's league. So, join a hockey team today for fun and fitness! And remember, if there isn't a hockey team in your neighborhood or at your school, you can always start your own. I guarantee it'll be one of the best experiences of your life.

LIST OF ADDRESSES

CANADIAN HOCKEY NATIONAL OFFICES

Canadian Hockey
1600 prom. James Naismith Dr.,
Suite 607
Gloucester, ON K1B 5N4
(613) 748-5613 fax: (613) 748-5709
www.canadianhockey.ca

Canadian Hockey
Father David Bauer Arena
2424 University Drive NW
Calgary, AB T2N 3Y9
(403) 777-3636 fax: (403) 777-3635

Independent Hockey Program
Olympic Oval Female Hockey Program
2500 University Drive NW
Calgary, AB T2N 1N4
(403) 220-7954 fax: (403) 284-4815

Alberta

Hockey Alberta
1-7875-48th Avenue
Red Deer, AB T4P 2K1
(403) 342-6777 fax: (403) 346-4277

British Columbia

BCAHA
6671 Oldfield Road
Saanichton, BC V8M 2A1
(250) 652-2978 fax: (250) 652-4536

Manitoba

Hockey Manitoba
200 Main Street
Winnipeg, MB R3C 4M2
(204) 925-5757 fax: (204) 925-5761

New Brunswick

NBAHA
165 Regent Street, Suite 4
Fredericton, NB E3B 4Z9
(506) 453-0098 fax: (506) 452-8088

Newfoundland

NAHA
15a High Street
P.O. Box 176
Grand Falls, NF A2A 2J4
(709) 489-5512 fax: (709) 489-2273

Nova Scotia

NSHA
6080 Young Street, Suite 910
Halifax, NS B3K 2A2
(902) 454-9400 fax: (902) 454-3883

Ontario

Ontario Hockey Federation
1185 Eglinton Avenue East, Suite 301
North York, ON M3C 3C6
(416) 426-7249 fax: (416) 426-7347

Ontario Women's Hockey Association
Unit 30, 1100 Central Parkway West
Mississauga, ON L5C 4E5
(905) 275-8866 fax: (905) 275-2001

**Thunder Bay Amateur Hockey
Association**
415 East Victoria Avenue
Thunder Bay, ON P7C 1A6
(807) 622-4792 fax: (807) 623-0037

Ottawa District Hockey Association
1900 Merivale Road
Nepean, ON K2G 4N4
(613) 224-7686 fax: (613) 224-6079

Prince Edward Island

PEIHA
68 University Avenue
Charlottetown, PEI C1A 4L1
(902) 566-5171 fax: (902) 894-5412

Quebec

Quebec Ice Hockey Federation
4545, av. Pierre-de-Coubertin
C.P. 1000 Succursale M
Montreal, QC H1V 3R2
(514) 252-3079 fax: (514) 252-3158

Saskatchewan

SAHA
1844 Victoria Avenue East
Regina, SK S4N 7K3
(306) 789-5101 fax: (306) 789-6112

Northwest Territories

NTAHA
P.O. Box 296
Fort Smith, NWT X0E 0P0
(867) 872-2342 fax: (867) 872-4730

CENTER OF EXCELLENCE LOCATIONS

Centre of Excellence — Toronto
BCE Place, 30 Yonge Street
Toronto, ON M5E 1X8
(416) 360-8432 fax: (416) 360-1316

Centre of Excellence — Calgary
Olympic Saddledome
P.O. Box 1060
Calgary, AB T2P 2K2
(403) 777-3644 fax: (403) 777-3641

Centre of Excellence — Atlantic
Suite 150, Building C
Hilyard Place, 600 Main Street
Saint John, NB E2K 1J5
(506) 652-8494 fax: (506) 652-6641

Centre of Excellence — Vancouver
B.C. Centre of Excellence
GM Place, 800 Griffiths Way
Vancouver, BC V6B 6G1
(604) 899-7770 fax: (604) 899-7771

CAAWS

**Canadian Association for the
Advancement of Women in Sport and
Physical Activity**
1600 James Naismith Drive
Gloucester, ON K1B 5N4
(613) 748-5793 fax: (613) 748-5775

CANADIAN COLLEGE ATHLETIC ASSOCIATION

Universities and Colleges (*indicates a varsity program)

Acadia University
Athletic Department
Wolfville, NS B0P 1X0
(902) 542-2200, ext.1427

University of Alberta*
University of Alberta Pandas
Women's Hockey Coach
87th Avenue & 114 Street
Edmonton, AB T6G 2E9
(403) 492-3080

Bishop's University*
Women's Hockey Coach
Lennoxville, QC J1M 1Z7
(819) 562-8202

Brandon University
Athletic Department
20th & Louise
Brandon, MB R7A 6A9
(204) 727-7431

University of British Columbia*
UBC Thunderbirds
Women's Hockey Coach
272-6081 University Blvd.
Vancouver, BC V6T 1W5
(604) 221-8077

Brock University
Athletic Department
St. Catharines, ON L2S 3A1
(905) 688-5550, ext. 4368

University of Calgary*
Women's Hockey Coach
2500 University Drive NW
Calgary, AB T2N 1N4
(403) 220-3424

University College of Cape Breton
Athletic Department
P.O. Box 5300
Sydney, NS B1P 6L2
(902) 562-1344

Concordia University*
Concordia Stingers
Women's Hockey Coach
7141 Sherbrooke Street West
Montreal, QC H4B 1R6
(514) 848-3865

Dalhousie University
Athletic Department
Dalplex South Street
Halifax, NS B3H 3J5
(902) 425-4874

University of Guelph*
Guelph Gryphons
Women's Hockey Coach
Guelph, ON N1G 2W1
(519) 824-4120, ext. 8785

Lakehead University
Athletic Department
955 Oliver Road
Thunder Bay, ON P7B 5E1
(807) 343-8605

Laurentian University
Athletic Department
935 Ramsey Lake Road
Sudbury, ON P3E 2C6
(705) 675-1151, ext.1025

Université Laval*
Women's Hockey Coach
Laval Rouge
Cité Universitaire, QC G1K 7P4
(418) 656-3268

University of Lethbridge
Women's Hockey Coach
4401 University Drive
Lethbridge, AB T1K 3M4
(403) 329-2380

University of Manitoba*
Lady Bisons
Women's Hockey Coach
236 Beliveau Road
Winnipeg, MB R2M 1T4
(204) 253-1178

McGill University*
McGill Martlets
Women's Hockey Coach
475 Pine Avenue West
Montreal, QC H2W 1S4
(514) 398-7003

McMaster University*
McMaster Marauders
Women's Hockey Coach
1280 Main Street West
Hamilton, ON L8S 4K1
(905) 526-1573

Memorial University of Newfoundland*
Memorial Sea-Hawks
Women's Hockey Coach
Elizabeth Avenue
St. John's, NF A1C 5S7
(709) 376-5254

Université de Moncton
Athletic Department
Moncton, NB E1A 3E9
(506) 858-4165

Mount Allison University
Athletic Department
Sackville, NB E0A 3C0
(506) 364-2405

University of New Brunswick
Athletic Department
P.O. Box 4400
Fredericton, NB E3B 5A3
(506) 536-0012

University of Ottawa
Athletic Department
Montpetit Hall
125 University Street
Ottawa, ON K1N 6N5
(613) 564-2454

University of Prince Edward Island
Athletic Department
University Avenue
Charlottetown, PEI C1A 4P3
(902) 566-0432

Université du Quèbec à Trois-Rivières
Athletic Department
CP 500, Pavillon des Sports
Parc de l'exposition
Trois-Rivières, QC G9A 5H7
(819) 376-5254

Queen's University*
Queen's Golden Gaels
Women's Hockey Coach
Physical Education Centre
Union Street
Kingston, ON K7L 3N6
(613) 545-6000, ext. 4731

University of Regina
Regina Cougars
Athletic Department
Regina, SK S4S 0A2
(306) 585-5010

Royal Military College of Canada
Athletic Department
Kingston, ON K7K 5L0
(613) 547-6263

Ryerson Polytechnic University
Athletic Department
350 Victoria Street
Toronto, ON M5B 2K3
(416) 979-5340, ext. 6123

St. Francis Xavier University
Athletic Department
P.O. Box 5000
Antigonish, NS B2G 2W5
(902) 867-2239

Saint Mary's University
Athletic Department
Halifax, NS B3H 3C3
(902) 420-5429

St. Thomas University
Athletic Department
Fredericton, NB E3B 5G3
(506) 452-7700

University of Saskatchewan*
Saskatchewan Huskies
Women's Hockey Coach
105 Gymnasium Place
Saskatoon, SK S7N 5C2
(306) 966-6490

University of Toronto*
Toronto Varsity Blues
Women's Hockey Coach
Department of Athletics and Recreation
55 Harbord Street
Toronto, ON M5S 2W6
(416) 978-3443

University of Waterloo
Athletic Department
University Avenue
Waterloo, ON N2L 3G1
(519) 885-1211, ext. 2635

University of Western Ontario
Athletic Department
Richmond Street North
London, ON N6A 3K7
(519) 661-3551, ext. 8392

Wilfrid Laurier University*
Women's Hockey Coach
75 University Avenue West
Waterloo, ON N2L 3C5
(519) 884-1970, ext. 2384

University of Windsor*
Athletic Department
Windsor, ON N9B 3P4
(519) 253-4232, ext. 2437

York University*
York Yeowomen
Women's Hockey Coach
4700 Keele Street
North York, ON M3J 1P3
(416) 736-5200

USA HOCKEY INC., GIRLS'/WOMEN'S SECTION COMMITTEE MEMBERS, 1997–1998

USA Hockey Inc.
1775 Bob Johnson Drive
Colorado Springs, CO 80906-4090
(719) 576-8724 fax: (719) 538-1160
www.usahockey.com

Girls'/Women's Section Director
Karen Lundgren
15868 Silver Lake Lane
Addison, MI 49220
(517) 547-6565 fax: (517) 547-3066

Atlantic

Delaware, Eastern Pennsylvania, New Jersey
Jayne McDonald
497 Golden Gate Road
Richboro, PA 18954
(215) 942-7979 fax: (215) 942-7977

Central

Illinois, Iowa, Kansas, Missouri, Nebraska, Wisconsin
Judy Ferwerda
264 Grand Canyon Drive
Madison, WI 53705
(608) 829-1449 fax: (608) 829-1449

Massachusetts
Carl Gray
43 Riverdale Rd.
Concord, MA 01742
(508) 369-5369 fax: (508) 369-8282
rink: (508) 369-8100
e-mail: assabetgrl@aol.com

Michigan
Sue McDowell
6514 Crane Rd.
Ypsilanti, MI 48197
(734) 528-0644
e-mail: gocoach@umich.edu

Minnkota

Minnesota, North Dakota, South Dakota
Lynn Olson
5909 12th Avenue S.
Minneapolis, MN 55417
(612) 861-2761 (phone/fax)

New England

Connecticut, Maine, New Hampshire, Rhode Island, Vermont
Alix Morin
5 Aspetuck Hill
Weston, CT 06883
(203) 222-1017
e-mail: mdnf90a@prodigy.com, or
www.nedistrict.com

New York

Nancy Denicola-March
P.O. Box 6424
Watertown, NY 13601

Mid-American

Indiana, Kentucky, Ohio, Western Pennsylvania, West Virginia
Barbara Williams
1217 Hunter Ridge Ct.
Evansville, IN 47711
(812) 867-1712
e-mail: courtplay@aol.com

Pacific

California, Nevada, Northern Idaho, Oregon, Washington
Robin Willins
973 Sudden Valley
Bellingham, WA 98226
(360) 733-0481 fax: (360) 734-3502
e-mail: willins@msn.com

Rocky Mountain

Arizona, Colorado, Montana, New Mexico, Oklahoma, Southern Idaho, Texas, Utah, Wyoming
Bruce Karinen
6379 Senoma Drive
Salt Lake City, UT 84121-2264
(801) 278-8865 fax: (801) 278-6914

Southeastern

Alabama, Arkansas, District of Columbia, Florida, Georgia, Louisiana, Maryland, Mississippi, North Carolina, South Carolina, Tennessee, Virginia

Kush Sidhu
Rinksport Entertainment
10166 Treble Court
Rockville, MD 20850
(301) 279-0919 fax: (301) 738-3737
e-mail: rinksprt@erols.com

Youth Council Chairman

John Dotte
P.O. Box 473
Ft. Covington, NY 12937
(518) 358-2591 fax: (518) 358-4290

President, American Women's Hockey Coaches Association

Julie Andeberhan
Cornell Hockey
Teagle Hall, Campus Rd.
Ithaca, NY 14853
(607) 255-6675 fax: (607) 255-2969
e-mail: jea5@cornell.edu

U.S. WOMEN'S COLLEGE AND UNIVERSITY HOCKEY PROGRAMS
(*indicates a varsity program)

Amherst College*
Department of Athletics
P.O. Box 5000, Alumni Gym
Amherst, MA 01002-5000
(413) 542-2219 fax: (413) 542-2026
e-mail: kbcowperthwa@amherst.edu

Augsburg College*
Athletic Director
2211 Riverside Ave., CB 279
Minneapolis, MN 55454
(612) 330-1377 fax: (612) 330-1372
e-mail: pohtilla@augsburg.edu

Bates College*
Athletic Director
Box 189
Lewiston, ME 04240
(207) 786-6345 fax: (207) 786-8232
e-mail: hdalglei@abacus.bates.edu

Boston College*
Athletic Director
321 Conte Forum, Suite 411
Chestnut Hill, MA 02167
(617) 552-3104 fax: (617) 552-4903
e-mail: o'malleyt@bc.edu

Boston University
Athletic Director
285 Babcock Street
Boston, MA 02215
(617) 353-2748 fax: (617) 353-5147
e-mail: seanob@ix.netcom.com

Bowdoin College*
Athletic Director
Morrell Gym, Bowdoin College
Brunswick, ME 04011
(207) 725-3893 fax: (207) 725-3019
e-mail: fquistga@henry.bowdoin.edu

Bowling Green State University
Athletic Director
1451 Clough St., #305A
Bowling Green, OH 43402
(419) 352-3382
e-mail: afickel@bgnet.bgsu.edu
e-mail: wellman@bgnet.bgsu.edu

Brown University*
Athletic Director
Brown University
P.O. Box 1847, Meehan Auditorium
Providence, RI 02912
(401) 863-3704 fax: (401) 863-3409
e-mail: margaret_murphy@brown.edu

Carleton College
Athletic Director
Cowling Recreation Center
300 North College Street
Northfield, MN 55057
(507) 646-4965
e-mail: Jdavis@carleton.edu
e-mail: traftonk@carleton.edu

Chatham College*
Athletic Department
Woodland Road
Pittsburg, PA 15232
(412) 365-1265 fax: (412) 365-1724
e-mail: omalley@chatham.edu

Clarkson University
Athletic Director
CU Box 3362
Potsdam, NY 13699-3349
(315) 265-5937
e-mail: clabouas@fire.clarkson.edu
e-mail: wareincm@polaris.clarkson.edu

Colby College*
Athletic Director
Colby College Athletic Dept.
4900 Mayflower Hill
Waterville, ME 04901
(207) 872-3079 fax: (207) 872-3420
e-mail: jlholste@colby.edu

Colgate University
Athletic Department
13 Oak Dr.
Hamilton, NY 13346
(315) 824-7060 fax: (315) 824-7925
e-mail: bhouston@center.colgate.edu

Colorado College
Athletic Department
CC El Pomar Center
902 North Cascade
Colorado Springs, CO 80903
(719) 389-6475 fax: (719) 389-6873
e-mail: M_king@cc.colorado.edu

University of Colorado — Boulder
Athletic Director, CU Club Sports
Campus Box 355
Boulder, CO 80309
(303) 492-5133 fax: (303) 492-7430

University of Connecticut
Athletic Department
2095 Hillside Road
Storrs, CT 06269
(860) 486-3059 fax: (860) 486-5085

Connecticut College*
Athletic Director
270 Mohegan Ave., Box 5245
New London, CT 06320-4196
(860) 439-2847 fax: (860) 439-2516
e-mail: mmdav@conncoll.edu

Cornell University*
Athletic Director, Julie Andeberhan
Teagle Hall, Campus Road
P.O. Box 729
Ithaca, NY 14853
(607) 255-6675 fax: (607) 255-2969
e-mail: jea5@cornell.edu

Dartmouth College*
Athletic Director
Dartmouth College
Alumni Gym Box 6083
Hanover, NH 03755-3512
(603) 646-2774 fax: (603) 646-3348
e-mail: George.E.Crowe@dartmouth.edu

Gustavus Adolphus College*
Athletic Director
800 West College Avenue
St. Peter, MN 56082-1498
(507) 933-7610
fax: (507) 933-8412
e-mail: smoe@gac.edu

Hamilton College*
Athletic Department
196 College Hill Road
Clinton, NY 13323
(315) 859-4758 fax: (315) 859-4117

Harvard University*
Athletic Director
Harvard University
60 John F. Kennedy Street
Cambridge, MA 02138
(617) 495-2281 fax: (617) 496-9343
e-mail: kbstone@fas.harvard.edu

Holy Cross
Athletic Director, Student Activities
1 College Street
Worcester, MA 01610
(508) 793-3487

University of Illinois — Champaign
Athletic Director
170 IMPE Bldg.
201 Peabody Drive
Champaign, IL 61820
(217) 351-4350 fax: (217) 244-3269

Iowa State University
Athletic Director
Maple 4146 Hayden
Ames, IA 50013-0011
(515) 294-3820
e-mail: roobie@iastate.edu

Lake Forest College
Sport Center
555 North Sheridan
Lake Forest, IL 60045
(847) 234-7654 fax: (847) 735-6290

University of Maine*
Athletic Director
328 Dunn Hall
Orono, ME 04469

Mankato State*
Athletic Director
MSU 28, P.O. Box 8400
Mankato, MN 56002-8400
(507) 645-4969
e-mail: todd.carroll@mankato.msus.edu

University of Massachusetts at Amherst
Athletic Director
Box 144, RSO Office-Student Union
Amherst, MA 01003
(413) 545-6531
e-mail: whockey@stuaf.umass.edu

Massachusetts Institute of Technology (MIT)
P.O. Box D, Athletic Department
77 Massachusetts Ave.
Cambridge MA 02139
(617) 253-4498
e-mail: jill@mit.edu

Michigan State University
Athletic Director
MSU Women's Ice Hockey, Munn Ice Arena
P.O.Box 6296
East Lansing, MI 48823
(517) 336-5593
e-mail: mandoros@pilot.msu.edu

Western Michigan
Athletic Director
Kalamzoo, MI
(616) 387-9583

Michigan Tech University
106 Memorial Union Building
1503 Townsend Dr.
Houghton, MI 49931
(906) 487-2406

University of Michigan
Athletic Director
NCRB — 2376 Hubbard
Ann Arbor, MI 48109
(313) 763-4560 fax: (313) 936-0604
e-mail: megreen@umich.edu

Middlebury College*
Athletic Director
Memorial Field House
Middlebury, VT 05753
(802) 443-5398 fax: (802) 443-2073
e-mail:
Mandigo_bill@msmail.middlebury.edu

University of Minnesota — Twin Cities
221 Cooke Hall
1900 University Avenue SE
Minneapolis, MN 55455
(612) 625-6017 fax: (612) 626-7708
e-mail: wohkyclb@tc.umn.edu

University of Minnesota — Twin Cities*
Athletic Director
250 BFAB
516-15th Ave., SE
Minneapolis, MN 55455
(612) 626-1770 fax: (612) 626-0020
e-mail:
Laura.M.Halldorson-1@tc.umn.edu

University of Minnesota — Duluth*
Athletic Director
10 University Dr., 121 SPHC
Duluth, MN 55812
(218) 726-8868 fax: (218) 726-6331
e-mail: kparr@d.umn.edu

Mount Holyoke College
Athletic Director
1989 Blanchard Student Center
South Hadley, MA 01075
(413) 538-2539

University of New Hampshire*
Athletic Director
Field House, Towse Rink
Whittemore Center
Durham, NH 03824
(603) 862-1161 fax: (603) 862-17411
e-mail: kak@hopper.unh.edu

Niagara University*
Women's Hockey Office
Niagara University, NY 14109-2009
(716) 286-8781 fax: (716) 286-8785
e-mail: mpage@niagara.edu

North County Community College
Athletic Director
20 Winona Avenue
Saranc Lake, NY 12983
(518) 891-2915 fax: (518) 891-2916,
ext. 214
e-mail: eileendg@aol.com

Northeastern University*
Athletic Director
Matthews Arena Annex
238 St. Botolph Street
Boston, MA 02115
(617) 373-4772 fax: (617) 373-8772
e-mail: hlinstad@lynx.neu.edu

Ohio State University
Athletic Director
106 Larkens Hall
Columbus, OH 43210
(937) 342-0983
e-mail: bradbury.5@osu.edu

University of Pennsylvania
Athletic Director
Gimbel Gym, 3701 Walnut Street
Philadelphia, PA 19104
(215) 573-8311

Penn State University
Athletic Director
14 Greenberg Sports Complex
University Park, PA 16802-1217
(814) 863-2039
e-mail: vxs7@emall.psu.edu

Princeton University*
Athletic Director
Baker Rink, CN 5283, P.O. Box 71
Jadwin Gym — Rm.#9
Princeton, NJ 08543
(609) 258-5975 fax: (609) 258-6676
e-mail: jkampy@arelia.princeton.edu

Providence College*
Sports Information Director
Athletic Department, River Arena
Providence College, Alumni Hall
Providence, Rhode Island 02918
(401) 865-2291 fax: (401) 865-1231
e-mail: jbarto@providence.edu

Rensselaer Polytechnic Institute*
Houston Field House
110 8th Street
Troy, NY 12180
(518) 276-2192 fax: (518) 276-8669
e-mail: stoner2@rpi.edu

Rochester Institute of Technology*
Sports Information Director
P.O. Box 9887, Clark Gym
51 Lamb Memorial Drive
Rochester, NY 14623
(716) 475-7148 fax: (716) 475-5675

Sacred Heart University*
Athletic Director
5151 Park Ave.
Fairfield, CT 06432
(203) 365-7526 fax: (203) 365-7696
e-mail: bourgett@sacredheart.edu

Skidmore College
Athletic Department
Sports Center, North Broadway
Sarasota Springs, NY 12666
(518) 584-2259 fax: (518) 584-3023

Smith College
Athletic Director
98 Green St., SC Box 7178
Northhampton, MA 01063
(413) 585-6930
e-mail: dyoung@otelia.smith.edu

University of Southern Maine*
Athletic Director
USM Hill Gymnasium
37 College Avenue
Gorham, ME 04038
(207) 780-5996
e-mail: abeaney@usm.maine.edu

College of St. Benedict*
CSB Athletic Department
37 South College Avenue
St. Joseph, MN 56374-2099
(320) 363-5873 fax: (320) 363-6098
e-mail: bkelly@csbsju.edu

St. Catherines* and St. Thomas*
Athletic Director
6115 26th St. North
Oakdale, MN 55812
(612) 773-0271
e-mail: sfbrown@alex.stkate.edu
e-mail: joandregg@stthomas.edu

St. Cloud State University
Women's Hockey Coach
1217 4th Avenue South, #204
St. Cloud, MN 56301
(320) 253-2355
e-mail:
womhock@condor.st.cloud.msus.edu

St. Lawrence University*
Augsbury PE Center
Canton, NY 13617
(315) 229-5740 fax: (315) 229-5589
e-mail: rwas@music.stlawu.edu

St. Mary's*
Athletic Director
700 Terrace Heights, #163
Winona, MN 55987
(507) 457-1976
e-mail: JCBAUER@rex.smumn.edu

St. Olaf College*
Athletic Director
1500 St Olaf Ave.
Northfield, MN 55057-1001
(507) 646-2222
e-mail: keith@stolaf.edu

Syracuse
Athletic Director
University Ave.
Syracuse, NY 13201
(315) 443-6280
e-mail: sltrahan@mailbox.syr.edu

Trinity College
Athletic Director
Ferris Athletic Center
Hartford, CT 06106
(860) 297-2062
e-mail:
Chantal.Lacroix@mail.trincoll.edu

Union College
Athletic Director
Box 2145
807 Union Street
Schenectady, NY 12308
(518) 388-7035
e-mail: stvrain@idol.union.edu

University of Vermont
284 East Avenue
Box 50501
Burlington, VT 05405
(802) 656-2186 fax: (802) 656-1075
e-mail: dennism@ppvax.uvm.edu

Wesleyan University*
Freeman Athletic Center
Middletown, CT 08459
(860) 685-2904 fax: (860) 685-2691
e-mail: dmattson@wesleyan.edu

Western Michigan University
Athletic Director
Lawson Ice Arena
Kalamazoo, MI 49008
(616) 388-4272

Wheaton College
Athletic Director
Evelyn D. Haas Athletic Center
Norton, MA 02766
(401) 245-3617
e-mail: smo2@ids.net

William Smith College
P.O. Box 265
Geneva, NY 14456
(315) 781-1520

University of Wisconsin — Stevens Point
Campus Activity Office
Box 23 Stevens Point, WI 544811
(715) 342-3685
e-mail: palvi492@uwsp.edu

University of Wisconsin — Madison
Athletic Director
7329 Timberlake Trail
Madison, WI 53719
(608) 273-8743
e-mail: anderson@monsters.com

University of Wisconsin — Eau Claire
Athletic Director
502 ½ Union Street
Eau Claire, WI 54703
(715)835-4994
e-mail: berndtcl@uwec.edu

University of Wisconsin — River Falls
Athletic Director
112 South 3rd Street
River Falls, WI 54022
(715) 426-9889 fax: (715) 426-9958
e-mail: rm16@uwrf.edu

University of Wisconsin — Whitewater
Athletic Director
800 West Main Street
Whitewater WI 531190
(414) 473-6579
e-mail: helgesonjm27@uwwvax.uww.edu

Yale University *
Hockey Information Director
Yale University
Box 208216
New Haven, CT 06520-8216
(203) 432-1457 fax: (203) 432-7772

FURTHER READING

Avery, Joanna and Julie Stevens. *Too Many Men on the Ice: Women's Hockey in North America*. Vancouver: Polestar Press, 1997.

Dryden, Ken and Roy MacGregor. *Home Game: Hockey and Life in Canada*. Toronto: McClelland and Stewart, 1989.

Etue, Elizabeth and Megan K. Williams. *On the Edge: Women Making Hockey History*. Toronto: Second Story Press, 1996.

McFarlane, Brian. *Proud Past, Bright Future: One Hundred Years of Canadian Women's Hockey*. Toronto: Stoddart Publishing, 1994.

Rhéaume, Manon with Chantal Gilbert. *Manon: Alone in Front of the Net*. Toronto: HarperCollins, 1993.

Young, Ian and Chris Gudgeon. *Behind the Mask: The Ian Young Goaltending Method, Book One*. Vancouver: Polestar Press, 1992.

Young, Ian and Chris Gudgeon. *Beyond the Mask: The Ian Young Goaltending Method, Book Two*. Vancouver: Polestar Press, 1993.

GLOSSARY

Assist: Point awarded to a player or players for helping set up a goal; usually the last two players to handle the puck.

Backchecking: When forwards attempt to regain control of the puck in their defensive zone.

Boards: The wooden and glass walls that surround the rink.

Breakaway: A scoring opportunity that occurs when there are no defending players between the puck carrier and the opposing goaltender.

Breakout: When the offensive team leaves its defensive zone with the puck and starts up the ice.

Changing on the Fly: Substitution of players without a stoppage in play.

Crease: The area in front of the goal marked off by a thin red line. In some cases the crease is light blue in colour.

Drop Pass: When the puck carrier leaves the puck behind to be picked up by a trailing teammate.

Face-Off: The action of an official dropping the puck between the sticks of two opposing players to start play.

Forechecking: Pressuring the opponent when they control the puck in the neutral or defensive zone in an effort to regain control of the puck.

Icing the Puck: When the puck is shot by one team from behind the center ice red line and crosses the opponent's goal line without a player touching the puck or the puck going through the goaltender's crease.

Hat Trick: Three goals scored by one player in a single game.

Neutral Zone: Center ice between attacking and defending zones (between blue lines).

Offsides: When an attacking player precedes the puck (crosses the blue line) into their offensive zone.

Penalty Box: Off-ice area at center ice where penalized players serve their time.

Point: A position just inside the blue line and close to the boards that attacking defensemen usually take when their team is in control of the puck in their offensive zone.

Poke Check: Causing the puck carrier to lose control of the puck by dislodging it with the blade of the stick.

Power Play: When a team has more players on the ice because of a penalty (or penalties) called against the opposing team.

Pull the Goalie: In an attempt to tie the score, a team trailing by one or two goals may take its goalie off the ice and send on an extra skater. This usually occurs in the closing minutes of a game.

Screenshot: A shot on goal when one or more players block the goaltender's view of the shot.

Shorthanded: When a team is forced to play with fewer than six players because one or more have been sent to the penalty box.

Stick-Handling: Using the stick to advance the puck along the ice.

PENALTY BOX

Boarding: Checking an opponent into the boards.

Butt-Ending: Using the shaft of the stick above the upper hand to jab or attempt to jab an opposing player.

Checking from Behind: Making physical contact with an opponent from directly behind.

Cross-Checking: Holding the stick with both hands to hit an opponent.

Elbowing: Making contact with an opponent with the elbow extended.

High-Sticking: Making contact with an opponent with a stick that is held above the shoulders.

Holding: Using the hands, arms, or legs to impede the progress of an opponent.

Hooking: Applying the blade of the stick to any part of the opponent's body or stick to impede her progress by a pulling or tugging motion with the stick.

Interference: To hinder or restrain a player not immediately involved in playing the puck.

Roughing: Any punch, push, or other unnecessary contact with an opponent.

Slashing: Striking or attempting to strike an opponent with a stick or swinging a stick at an opponent with no contact being made. Tapping an opposing player's stick is not considered slashing.

Spearing: Poking or attempting to poke an opponent with the tip of the blade of the stick.

Tripping: Using the stick, leg, foot, or other body part to cause an opponent to trip or fall.